California Bar Examination

Essay Questions and Selected Answers

July 2016

The State Bar Of California
Committee of Bar Examiners/Office of Admissions

180 Howard Street • San Francisco, CA 94105-1639 • (415) 538-2300
845 S. Figueroa Street • Los Angeles, CA 90017-2515 • (213) 765-1500

ESSAY QUESTIONS AND SELECTED ANSWERS

JULY 2016

CALIFORNIA BAR EXAMINATION

This publication contains the six essay questions from the July 2016 California Bar Examination and two selected answers for each question.

The answers were assigned high grades and were written by applicants who passed the examination after one read. The answers were produced as submitted by the applicant, except that minor corrections in spelling and punctuation were made for ease in reading. They are reproduced here with the consent of the authors.

Question Number	Subject
1.	Civil Procedure
2.	Real Property
3.	Contracts
4.	Constitutional Law
5.	Community Property
6.	Professional Responsibility

ESSAY EXAMINATION INSTRUCTIONS

Your answer should demonstrate your ability to analyze the facts in the question, to tell the difference between material facts and immaterial facts, and to discern the points of law and fact upon which the case turns. Your answer should show that you know and understand the pertinent principles and theories of law, their qualifications and limitations, and their relationships to each other.

Your answer should evidence your ability to apply the law to the given facts and to reason in a logical, lawyer-like manner from the premises you adopt to a sound conclusion. Do not merely show that you remember legal principles. Instead, try to demonstrate your proficiency in using and applying them.

If your answer contains only a statement of your conclusions, you will receive little credit. State fully the reasons that support your conclusions, and discuss all points thoroughly.

Your answer should be complete, but you should not volunteer information or discuss legal doctrines that are not pertinent to the solution of the problem.

Unless a question expressly asks you to use California law, you should answer according to legal theories and principles of general application.

QUESTION 1

Paul, a citizen of Mexico, was attending college in San Diego on a student visa. He drove to San Francisco to attend a music festival. While there, he bought and ate a bag of snacks from Valerie, a resident of San Francisco. The snacks had been manufactured in Germany by Meyer Corp., a German company with its sole place of business in Germany. The snacks contained a toxic substance and sickened Paul, who incurred medical expenses in the amount of $50,000.

Paul filed an action pro se against Valerie and Meyer Corp. in the Superior Court of California in San Diego. In his complaint, he alleged that Valerie and Meyer Corp. should have known the snacks were contaminated and demanded $50,000 in compensatory damages.

Paul drove to San Francisco where he personally handed Valerie a summons and copy of the complaint. He sent a summons and copy of the complaint to Meyer Corp. by ordinary mail to the company in Germany.

1. Did Paul validly serve the summons on:

   a. Valerie? Discuss.

   b. Meyer Corp.? Discuss.

2. Does the Superior Court of California in San Diego have personal jurisdiction over:

   a. Valerie? Discuss.

   b. Meyer Corp.? Discuss.

3. Does venue properly lie in the Superior Court of California in San Diego? Discuss.

4. Is Paul's action properly removable to federal court? Discuss.

QUESTION 1: SELECTED ANSWER A

I. Service of Process

The issue is whether Paul properly served process over Valerie and Meyer Corp.

Service of process in California can be accomplished in a variety of ways. First and foremost, a defendant may be personally served with a summons and a copy of a complaint. When in-person service does not work, substituted service may be attempted by leaving the summons and a copy of the complaint with the defendant's registered agent or another person who resides at the defendant's domicile. The summons and complaint must also be sent via certified mail to the defendant's address of record. However, process must be served by a person over the age of 18 who is not a party to the case.

A. Valerie

Here, Paul personally served Valerie with process. Paul might be over the age of 18, but he is a party to the case and therefore cannot properly effect service himself. Though service by handing the defendant process personally is proper, Paul was not a proper process server. Accordingly, Paul did not validly serve process on Valerie.

B. Meyer Corp.

Paul's service of Meyer Corp. suffers from the same defect as his service of Valerie: he is not a proper process server because he is a party to the case. Additionally, service of process on an international is subject to different rules: process may be served either in compliance with governing international treaties, or via certified mail with a return receipt.

Here, Paul mailed the complaint via ordinary mail, rather than certified mail. Further, there does not appear to be an international treaty governing service of process. Accordingly, Paul cannot have validly served process using ordinary mail; he did not validly serve process on Meyer Corp.

II. Personal Jurisdiction

The issue is whether the San Diego Superior Court has personal jurisdiction over Valerie and Meyer Corp.

In personam jurisdiction describes the personal jurisdiction of a court over the parties before it. There are three traditional bases of in personam jurisdiction: when a defendant consents to the court's jurisdiction, when a defendant is domiciled in the jurisdiction in which the court sits, and when a defendant is present in the jurisdiction and is properly served with process while present. When the traditional bases of in personam jurisdiction do not apply, a state long-arm statute may provide an alternative basis for jurisdiction.

A. Valerie

Here, Valerie appears to satisfy one of the traditional prongs of in personam jurisdiction. She is a resident of San Francisco, and so is domiciled in California and therefore subject to the personal jurisdiction of California state courts. While Paul personally served Valerie in San Francisco after driving there, this service of process was improper as discussed above. Nonetheless, because another of the traditional bases has been met, Valerie is properly subject to the San Diego Superior Court's personal jurisdiction.

B. Meyer Corp.

1. Traditional Bases

Here, Meyer Corp. does not appear to satisfy any of the traditional bases of in personam jurisdiction. It does not appear that it has consented to California state courts' jurisdiction. Further, it is domiciled only in Germany. Finally, Paul did not serve process on Meyer Corp. in state. Accordingly, none of the traditional bases apply.

2. Long-Arm Statute and Constitutional Limitations

However, California also has a state long-arm statute that may provide an alternative basis for personal jurisdiction. California's long-arm statute goes to the full extent of the federal Constitution, subject only to Due Process limitations. For a court's exercise of personal jurisdiction to comport with Due Process, the defendant must have sufficient minimum contacts with the jurisdiction, the exercise of jurisdiction must be related to the defendant's contacts, and the exercise of jurisdiction must not offend traditional notions of fair play and substantial justice.

a. Minimum Contacts

For a defendant to have sufficient minimum contacts with California, it must have purposefully availed itself of California, such that it was foreseeable that its minimum contacts would cause it to be haled into the California courts. In stream-of-commerce cases, purposeful availment consists of some action by the defendant deliberately targeting the jurisdiction. Here, it is not clear whether Meyer Corp. has purposefully availed itself of California, as it is incorporated in Germany, headquartered in Germany, and conducts all of its manufacturing in Germany. More information is needed into its distribution chains. For example, if Meyer Corp. specifically shipped its snacks to Valerie for distribution in San Francisco, then Meyer Corp. will have purposefully availed itself by intending that its products be sold in California. By contrast, if Valerie purchased the snacks in Germany and decided on her own volition to sell them in California, then Meyer Corp. will not have purposefully availed itself. In the absence of such evidence, it appears that Meyer Corp. does not have sufficient minimum contacts with California.

b. Relatedness

Relatedness is satisfied either in a specific sense when a cause of action arises out of a defendant's contacts with a jurisdiction, or more generally when a defendant is domiciled in a jurisdiction and is essentially "at home" in that jurisdiction. Here, Meyer Corp. is domiciled in Germany and conducts all of its activities in Germany. Accordingly, it is not "at home" in California and does not satisfy the general relatedness criteria. However, the action arises out of Meyer Corp.'s snacks being consumed in California. Accordingly, the specific relatedness criteria is met.

c. Fair Play and Substantial Justice

Even when a defendant has sufficient minimum contacts and relatedness is satisfied, the exercise of personal jurisdiction must not offend traditional notions of fair play and substantial justice. In considered whether the exercise of personal jurisdiction does so, a court considers a multitude of factors, including the plaintiff's interest in relief, the forum state's interest in providing a forum such that the plaintiff can seek redress, and whether other forums might be more appropriate. Here, Paul was sickened quite extensively and incurred substantial damages. He has a strong interest in relief. Further, California has a strong interest in providing a forum. Even though Paul is not a citizen of California, California nonetheless has an interest in making sure that contaminated food products are not distributed within the state. Finally, while Meyer Corp. might claim that Germany is a more appropriate forum, given that the snacks were manufactured there and it conducts all of its business there, California nonetheless may be more appropriate, given that Valerie, Meyer's co-defendant, is a citizen of California. Given that she ultimately sold the snacks to Paul and is being sued jointly with Meyer Corp., California is a more appropriate forum than Germany. Accordingly, a California court's exercise of personal jurisdiction over Meyer Corp. would not offend traditional notions of fair play and substantial justice.

Therefore, whether the San Diego Superior Court can properly exercise jurisdiction over

Meyer Corp. depends on whether Meyer Corp. has sufficient minimum contacts with California. While more evidence is needed, it does not appear that Meyer Corp. has purposefully availed itself of California, and therefore, the court cannot properly exercise personal jurisdiction.

III. Venue

The issue is whether venue properly lies in San Diego Superior Court.

Venue in California is organized by each of the 58 counties in the state. Different rules apply based on whether the action is a local action or a transitory action. Venue is proper in a local action, one involving real property, in the county in which the real property lies. For a transitory action, venue is generally proper in a California Superior Court in any county where any defendant resides. For contract actions, venue is additionally proper in the county where the contract was entered into and the county where the contract was expected to be performed. For tort actions, venue is proper in the county where the act or omission giving rise to the tort occurred. If no venue is proper following the application of these rules, then venue is proper in any county in which a court has personal jurisdiction over the defendants.

A. Residence

Here, the action at issue is a transitory action as it does not involve any real property. Therefore, venue is proper in any county in which a defendant resides. In this case, the two defendants Valerie and Meyer Corp. are residents of San Francisco County and Germany, respectively. Because only Valerie's residence, San Francisco, is a county within California, the first venue provision only provides that the Superior Court in San Francisco is a proper venue.

B. Tort Actions

Here, Paul's claim appears to be a tort claim: he appears to be arguing negligence on behalf of Valerie and Meyer Corp. in producing the snacks, or possibly strict products liability. Accordingly, the venue rules for tort actions may also provide an alternative basis for proper venue. In this case, the acts or omissions giving rise to Paul's action occurred in both San Francisco County, where Valerie sold him the snacks, and Germany, where the snacks were manufactured. Accordingly, under the analysis for a tort action, venue remains proper only in San Francisco.

C. Contract Actions

Paul could also plausibly allege that his action is a contract action, and that Valerie breached, for example, an implied warranty of fitness for a particular purpose when she sold him the snacks. Accordingly, venue is additionally proper in the county in which the contract was entered into, as well as the county in which the contract was expected to be performed. Here, both of those locations are the City and County of San Francisco: Paul agreed to purchase, and did purchase, the snacks from Valerie there. Accordingly, under the analysis for a contract action, venue is proper only in San Francisco.

D. Fallback Venue

Because venue is proper in at least one county in California, the fallback venue provision of any judicial district in which the court has personal jurisdiction over the defendant does not apply.

In conclusion, venue is only proper in San Francisco County Superior Court. Venue is not proper in San Diego Superior Court.

IV. Removal to Federal Court

The issue is whether Paul's action is properly removable to federal court.

A case initially filed in state court is properly removable to federal court when the case could originally have been brought in federal court. Removal is accomplished by filing a notice of removal in federal court within 30 days of service of a document that shows the case to be removable, but cases removable to federal court solely on the basis of federal diversity jurisdiction cannot be removed more than one year after the filing of the action in state court. Here, nothing indicates that Paul's case would be subject to these time restrictions. Accordingly, the issue is whether the case could have initially been brought in federal court.

For a case to be properly brought in federal district court, the federal court must have subject matter jurisdiction. A federal court may have federal question jurisdiction or diversity jurisdiction over a case. In cases where at least one "trunk" claim is within the court's federal question jurisdiction or diversity jurisdiction, the court may have jurisdiction over additional claims that share a common nucleus of operative fact with the federal trunk claim.

A. Federal Question Jurisdiction

Federal question jurisdiction consists of claims arising under the Constitution, treaties, and federal laws and regulations. The question must appear on the face of a well-pleaded complaint. Here, Paul does not appear to be asserting any federal rights. Unless he is asserting any causes of action under federal food safety regulations, for example, he appears solely to be asserting state-law tort claims -- that Valerie and Meyer Corp. were negligent in failing to detect that the snacks were contaminated. Accordingly, the federal court does not have federal question jurisdiction over Paul's action.

B. Diversity Jurisdiction

Diversity jurisdiction arises when there is a diversity of citizenship between the parties and the amount in controversy in the action exceeds $75,000.

1. Diversity of Citizenship

To satisfy diversity of citizenship, each plaintiff must be fully diverse from each defendant. A U.S. citizen or permanent resident alien is considered to be a citizen of the state in which she is domiciled, an alien is considered to be a citizen of the country of his citizenship, and a corporation is considered to be a citizen both of all jurisdictions in which it is incorporated and the state in which it has its principal place of business. However, even when each plaintiff is fully diverse from each defendant, a federal court still will not have subject matter jurisdiction if both the plaintiffs and defendants are aliens and U.S. citizens are not present on both sides of the action.

Here, Paul is not a permanent resident alien, as he is present in the country only on a student visa. Accordingly, for diversity jurisdiction purposes, he is a citizen of Mexico. Valerie resides in San Francisco, which is her domicile. Accordingly, for diversity purposes, Valerie is a citizen of California. Meyer Corp is incorporated in Germany only and has its principal place of business in Germany. Accordingly, Meyer Corp is a citizen of Germany.

Accordingly, the parties are fully diverse from each other: Paul does not share citizenship with either Valerie or Meyer Corp. However, the alienage restriction nonetheless bars Paul's action from satisfying the diversity requirements. Paul, as the only plaintiff, is an alien. Valerie is a U.S. citizen, but Meyer Corp. is also an alien, as it is only a citizen of Germany. Accordingly, aliens are present on both sides of the action, but U.S. citizens are not. Therefore, diversity of citizenship is not met.

2. Amount in Controversy

The amount in controversy is the amount, when plaintiff asserts a monetary damages claim, that a plaintiff seeks from the defendants. When a claim asserted jointly against two defendants, the amount in controversy is the total relief sought from the defendants. For a federal court to have jurisdiction, the amount in controversy must exceed $75,000.

Here, Paul seeks $50,000 in compensatory damages jointly from Valerie and Meyer Corp. Accordingly, the amount in controversy is $50,000, which does not exceed $75,000. Therefore, the amount in controversy requirement is also not met for diversity jurisdiction purposes.

Because neither the diversity of citizenship nor amount in controversy requirements are met, a federal district court would have not diversity jurisdiction over Paul's action. Accordingly, because a federal court has neither federal question jurisdiction nor diversity jurisdiction over Paul's action, it could not have originally been brought in federal district court. Therefore, Paul's action is not removable from California state court to federal district court.

QUESTION 1: SELECTED ANSWER B

1. SERVING A SUMMONS

A. WAS VALERIE SERVED PROPERLY

The issue is whether Paul properly served Valerie by personally handing her a summons and copy of the complaint.

PROPER SUMMONS

The Federal Rules of Civil Procedure allow for a party member to be served with process in a number of ways. One accepted method of service is personally serving the summons and complaint on the Defendant. A person may be served personally by any non-party who is 18 years or older. To effect proper service the Defendant should be given a summons and two copies of the complaint. Under California civil procedure, a person may similarly be personally served by a non-party 18 years or older by the same rules. This case has been filed in the superior court so it is under California rules. The CA rules prefer personal service.

In this case, Paul, a party to the case, drove to San Francisco where Valerie lived and handed her a summons and one copy of the complaint. This was improper. Paul was not allowed to serve Valerie because he is a party to the case. Further, there are no facts as to Paul's age, but service must be given by someone who is 18 years of age or older. Valerie was given one summons and one complaint. The rules require that Valerie be given two copies of the complaint. Because of this, service was not valid on Valerie.

B. WAS MEYER CORP SERVED PROPERLY

The issue is whether mailing a copy of the complaint and a summons by ordinary mail to Meyer Corp. in Germany was proper. The Federal Rules of Civil Procedure dictate that it is proper to serve a Defendant by mail. The summons and two copies of the complaint must be sent by first class mail, postage paid, with a waiver and a pre-addressed and prepaid envelope in which the Defendant can return the signed waiver. California rules of civil procedure also allow service by mail to a person out of the country in a similar manner. CA rules prefer personal service, but the California rules specifically say that a defendant who is out of the country may be served by mail according to the California rules. However, in CA (which governs in this case) the mailing of service is not technically a waiver as it is in federal court but it operates in the same manner.

In this case Paul sent a summons and a copy of the complaint to Meyer Corp. in Germany by ordinary mail. This was improper. First, the complaint needed to be sent with one summons and two copies of the complaint. It should have been sent by first class mail, postage paid, and should have included a form for the Defendant to sign with a pre-addressed and prepaid envelope to send the signed documents back to the plaintiff who will file them. Under the California rules, the mailing of a summons and complaint is not actually waiver (it is a form of service) but it operates like the federal waiver. Thus, Meyer Corp. was not properly served.

2. PERSONAL JURISDICTION

A. DOES THE SUPERIOR COURT OF CALIFORNIA HAVE PERSONAL JURISDICTION OVER VALERIE

Personal jurisdiction over the Defendant is required for a court to hear a case. It refers to the court having authority over the defendant. To have personal jurisdiction (PJ) over a defendant traditionally occurs when a Defendant is served with process while voluntarily in the state, the defendant is domiciled in the state, or the Defendant consents to the court exercising its power over him/her. If there is not a traditional basis for jurisdiction the court will look to see if there are minimum contacts with the forum state so as not to offend traditional notions of fair play and substantial justice. In evaluating this the court looks to three factors: (a) contacts with the forum state focusing on whether the defendant has purposeful availment and reasonably foresees being sued in the forum state; (b) Relatedness which occurs with general or specific jurisdiction in the forum state; and (c) fairness looking at if the defendant will be so gravely inconvenienced as to cause a substantial unfairness. The court will also look at the plaintiff's interests and the state's interest in effectuating justice under the fairness prong.

In this case Valerie is a resident of San Francisco. This means that Valerie is domiciled in California because she lives in a city (San Francisco) that is located in California. Therefore the court has personal jurisdiction over Valerie because she is domiciled in the forum state (California). Further, the court also has a traditional basis of jurisdiction over Valerie because she was personally served while voluntarily in California. Valerie was in San Francisco voluntarily because she lives there and was served with process while there. Thus, the court does have personal jurisdiction over Valerie according to two of the traditional bases of PJ.

B. DOES THE SUPERIOR COURT OF CALIFORNIA HAVE PJ OVER MEYER CORP

Personal jurisdiction over the Defendant is required for a court to hear a case. It refers to the court having authority over the defendant. To have personal jurisdiction (PJ) over a defendant traditionally occurs when a Defendant is served with process while voluntarily in the state, the defendant is domiciled in the state, or the Defendant consents to the court exercising its power over him/her. If there is not a traditional basis for jurisdiction the court will look to see if there are minimum contacts with the forum state so as not to offend traditional notions of fair play and substantial justice. In evaluating this the court looks to three factors: (a) contacts with the forum state focusing on whether the defendant has purposeful availment and reasonably foresees being sued in the forum state; (b) Relatedness which occurs with general or specific jurisdiction in the forum state; and (c) fairness looking at if the defendant will be so gravely inconvenienced as to cause a substantial unfairness. The court will also look at the plaintiff's interests and the states interest in effectuating justice under the fairness prong.

California's long-arm statute allows PJ over a defendant as long as it does not offend the constitution. Therefore the analysis of California's long-arm statute is merged with the constitutional analysis. The constitutional analysis is the minimum contacts test described above and analyzed below.

Meyer Corp. is a German company. It is incorporated in Germany with its sole place of business in Germany. Meyer Corp. was not served while voluntarily present in California. Further, there is no evidence that Meyer Corp. has consented to California having PJ over it. Because of this there is no traditional basis for personal jurisdiction. Therefore we must analyze PJ with the constitutional test of Minimum Contacts.

MINIMUM CONTACTS

There must be minimum contacts so as not to offend the traditional notions of fair play and substantial justice. This is analyzed looking at purposeful availment and foreseeability of being dragged into court.

PURPOSEFUL AVAILMENT

To have PJ Meyer Corp. must have purposefully availed itself into the forum state (CA) as such that it used the protections of its laws. In this case Meyer Corp. is a snack company. Its sole place of business is in Germany; however, the snack did get to California. If the company sold its products, advertised its products, or in some other way targeted California there will be purposeful availment. If Valerie brought these snacks back from Germany and the corp did not in any way reach out to CA, there will be no purposeful availment. There will be purposeful availment if Meyer Corp. directed sales to CA. It is unclear where and how Valerie came to get these snacks so the purposeful availment prong is unclear.

FORESEEABILITY

If Meyer Corp. did target CA in any way (by selling there, advertising there, selling candy to CA over the internet) then it is foreseeable that they would be sued there. If, though, Valerie got these snacks in Germany and then sold them when she was in California then it is not foreseeable that Corp. would be dragged into court in CA.

RELATEDNESS

If the defendant is essentially at home in the forum state there will be general jurisdiction. Corp. is located only in Germany with its sole place of business in Germany. Therefore no general jurisdiction.

If the defendant's contact with the forum state results in the cause of action there will be specific jurisdiction. This is unclear because we don't know if Corp. was in any way targeting to sell in California. If they were then specific jurisdiction, if not then no specific jurisdiction.

FAIRNESS

We look at if it is so gravely inconvenient that it will put Defendant at severe disadvantage. In this case Defendant is a corporation and monetary concerns are not good arguments. Therefore it is probably fair. Further CA has an interest in adjudicating for its citizens. Paul the plaintiff is in CA.

CONCLUSION

There is PJ over Valerie. PJ over Meyer depends on its operations and how the snack got into CA.

3. VENUE PROPER

Under CA civil procedure, venue depends on the type of action. If it is not a local action (land action where the venue is where the land is) then venue is where any defendant resides. Further for a personal injury case venue is proper where the injury took place.

This is a personal injury case because Paul was sickened. Therefore venue is proper in San Francisco (where injury took place) and in San Francisco (where a Defendant lives). Neither of the defendants lives in San Diego (Valerie lives in San Fran and Meyer lives in Germany). Therefore venue in San Diego was improper. Proper venue would be in San Francisco.

4. ACTION REMOVABLE?

An Action is removable to federal court when there is a federal question jurisdiction. This occurs when the plaintiff is enforcing a federal right - when the cause of action arises under federal law. In this case the cause of action arises under state law because it is a tort or personal injury action. There is no federal law at issue. Any federal defenses do not matter in determining whether there is federal question jurisdiction. Therefore action cannot be removed under federal question jurisdiction.

An action can also be removed if there is diversity jurisdiction. Diversity jurisdiction requires that there be complete diversity (no plaintiff can be a citizen of the same place as any defendant) and that the amount in controversy be in excess of $75,000. Further, an action cannot be removed if the defendant is a citizen in the same state as the action is brought. A plaintiff may aggregate her claims against multiple defendants if the defendants are jointly and severally liable.

In this case the amount in controversy is $50,000. Paul can assert this amount against both defendants because it is a case where he is saying both are jointly and severally liable for the entire amount. This amount is below the required $75,000 so there is no diversity jurisdiction. Further Valerie is a citizen of California because she is domiciled in CA. This means that Valerie is a citizen of the forum state - this prevents her from removing the case to federal court in CA because she is a citizen of CA. Further, the case cannot be removed because there are aliens on both sides of the case. Paul is a citizen of Mexico and is the plaintiff. Meyer is a citizen of Germany and is a defendant. We have an alien on each side which prevents diversity. To remedy this there must be diverse citizens of the United States on each side.

In conclusion, the action cannot be removed.

QUESTION 2

Al owned a farm.

In 1990, Al deeded an easement for a road along the north side of the farm to his neighbor Ben. Ben immediately graded and paved a road on the easement, but did not record the deed at that time. Al and Ben both used the road on a daily basis. The easement decreased the fair market value of the farm by $5,000.

In 2009, Al deeded the farm to his daughter Carol and she recorded the deed.

In 2011, Ben recorded his deed to the easement.

In 2012, Carol executed a written contract to sell the farm to Polly for $100,000. The contract stated in part: "Seller shall covenant against encumbrances with no exceptions." During an inspection of the farm, Polly had observed Ben traveling on the road along the north side of the farm, but said nothing.

In 2013, Carol deeded an easement for water lines along the south side of the farm to Water Co., the local municipal water company. The water lines provided water service to local properties, including the farm. Water Co. then recorded the deed. The easement increased the fair market value of the farm by $10,000.

In 2014, after long delay, Carol executed and delivered to Polly a warranty deed for the farm and Polly paid Carol $100,000. The deed contains a covenant against all encumbrances except for the easement to Water Co. and no other title covenants. Polly recorded the deed.

In 2015, Polly blocked Ben's use of the road and objected to Water Co.'s construction of the water lines.

Ben has commenced an action against Polly seeking declaratory relief that the farm is burdened by his easement. Polly in turn has commenced an action against Carol seeking damages for breach of contract and breach of the covenant under the warranty deed.

1. What is the likely outcome of Ben's action? Discuss.

2. What is the likely outcome of Polly's:

    a. Claim of breach of contract? Discuss.

       and

    b. Claim of breach of the covenant under the warranty deed? Discuss.

QUESTION 2: SELECTED ANSWER A

QUESTION ONE

At issue is the outcome of Ben's (B) action against Polly (P) for blocking the access to the road that he received an easement from Al (A) to use.

Express Easement

An easement is the right to enter onto someone's land and use a portion of that land for a specific purpose. Easements may be granted expressly to an individual by deed. An express easement by deed must meet the deed formalities to be valid, including a valid writing, and other statute of frauds requirements. Moreover easements are deemed to be perpetual in nature unless otherwise indicated. Here in 1990, A deeded an easement to B for using a road along the north side of his farm. There are no facts indicating whether or not the deed itself meets the formalities of a valid writing; however it can be presumed here because there are no facts to the contrary. Therefore given that A created an easement by deed, that expressly named the easement in the deed, an express easement was likely created for B's use. Thus in 1990, after A's valid deed, B obtained an express easement to use the road on the farm.

Reasonable Use/Scope

An easement must usually be used reasonably within the scope of the granting instrument if an express easement. This typically allows the holder of the easement to improve the land where the easement lies and to enter on to it to repair it. Here after A granted B the easement, B immediately graded and paved the road for his use. These actions are likely valid given that B was entering onto the property to pave a road. It would be implied that the holder of this easement for use of a road could enter onto land to improve the land, grade it and maintain the road. Therefore it would appear that B has been validly using the easement and comporting with its ramifications.

Termination

The next issue is whether B's easement could be said to have terminated in any way after P took title to the land it was on. Termination of an easement may occur where the easement is abandoned, where the granting instrument states a specific condition to occur, or where the properties that the easement lies on and the adjacent property holder are merged. Typically easements are perpetual in nature unless stated otherwise. Here A granted the easement to B by deed. There was nothing in the deed that stated any kind of condition as to whether the easement could terminate. Therefore no conditions have occurred. Moreover there was no abandonment of the easement as B has used the road ever since he was granted it. Finally no merger occurred under these facts as B still maintains his own property and the property that the easement lies on is separately owned by P now. Thus the easement did not terminate.

Transfer of Land - Notice

Generally when land that is burdened by the easement, the servient estate, transfers title the easement runs with the land. Thus even though A transferred the land to Carol (C) and then C transferred the land to P, each time the transfer occurred the easement would automatically run with the land. However a subsequent bona fide purchaser may attempt to argue that they lacked notice of the easement. If a subsequent bona fide purchaser can do so and state that they did not have notice of the easement then they can typically defeat an easement holder's title. The goal is to show that the subsequent bona fide purchaser did not have notice of the easement on the land. Thus P must show she did not have notice; this is done through a recording act.

Recording Act

Under the common law, title in land was measured by first in time, first in right. However under modern recording acts, people who record their interest in land can preserve their title by putting the world on notice of that interest in the land. There are jurisdictional splits as to what type of recording statute is used and there are three main ones: race, race-notice, and notice. Race recording statutes are used only in a minority of jurisdictions. Therefore notice and race-notice jurisdictions are typically the most commonly used. Here in order to use a recording statute, P would have to show that she was a SBP and that she met the requirements of each recording statute.

Subsequent Bona Fide Purchaser (SBP)

In order to actually argue that one did not have notice to the easement, they must be a SBP. Typically a SBP is someone who took title to land subsequently to the current holder of the land and they did so for value. Here P paid for title to the farm in which B's easement lies. Moreover B's interest was received in 1990 and P's interest was received in 2014, so she was subsequent.

Thus P is a SBP who could seek to use a recording statute to take superior title in land and invalidate B's easement.

Notice and Race-Notice Jurisdictions

In a notice jurisdiction and a race-notice jurisdiction, the SBP must show that at the time that they took title to the land they did not have a notice of the competing interest. There are three kinds of notice: inquiry, actual and constructive. Inquiry notice occurs where the SBP is charged with looking at the property to examine it, and if they had examined it they may have found the competing interest. Actual notice occurs where the SBP is actually aware of the interest and recording notice occurs where the competing interest was recorded so that the SBP was on constructive notice via the recording. Here P actually saw the road that B had built on the property and she saw that B was using it. Therefore P likely had actual notice since she physically saw someone driving on the land. Moreover B recorded his deed in 2011 and P did not record until 2014. Thus she would be on constructive notice as well. At a very minimum P should have asked C who B was and what he was doing. Therefore notice would most likely be charged to P.

Thus P as a SBP cannot argue that she took title to the land without notice of the competing interest.

Race Jurisdiction

In a race jurisdiction, the person who records first wins and that is why it is not used in many jurisdictions because it often results in unfair outcomes. Here B recorded in 2011 and P recorded in 2014. Thus under a race jurisdiction B would win as well.

Conclusion

In total, P cannot use a recording act to argue that she as a SBP should take title without B's interest. She had notice of B's usage of the land and moreover she did not record first. Thus the common law rule applies of first in time and first in right and B's interest is superior. P would lose to B's claim as B's easement would automatically run with the land.

Shelter Rule

Under the shelter rule, a SBP may be able to step into the shoes of a previous grantee and argue that the previous grantee could have validly used a recording in order to defeat a previous claim. The shelter rule may be used despite the fact that a SBP may have had actual knowledge. Here P could argue that C was a SBP under a recording act and therefore P could step into C's shoes to invalidate B's claim.

C as SBP

A SBP must typically pay value for title to the land and take subsequently to the competing interest. Here B got his easement in 1990 and C took title in 2009. Therefore C was subsequent. But it is not clear that C paid for the land. Her father was A and he just deeded her the land. If she did not pay value for the land then she was a mere donee and not a valid SBP. Any value is enough; typically only a "mere peppercorn" would suffice; but if someone did not actually give value then they are not a SBP. Thus if C was not a SBP then she could not use a recording act. As such it is unlikely that the shelter rule could be used here.

Recording Claim

Under a race notice and a notice jurisdiction it is likely that C would be charged with inquiry notice. Since B built and paved a road on the farm, that would have went from his farm to C's farm, any inspection of the farm that C was to take title to would charge with her inquiry notice. She would have seen the road and been charged with asking what it was. Moreover given B's usage of the road, she likely would have seen him, especially if this was her father's farm before it was hers. Thus under a race and race-notice jurisdiction it is unlikely that C would prevail since she likely took title with notice.

Under a race recording statute C would probably prevail however, since she did record before B did, as she recorded in 2011 and B recorded in 2014.

Conclusion - Shelter Rule

In total, P cannot likely use the shelter rule here to step into C's shoes because C was probably not a SBP. Moreover under a notice and race-notice recording statute she would not win since she probably would be charged with notice of B's claim. However she may win under a race recording statute if she was a SBP because she recorded first.

Overall Conclusion

In conclusion, B's claim against P would likely be valid. B can establish that he had a valid express easement and that it automatically ran with the land when it was transferred from A to C and then to P. Moreover P cannot argue she did not have notice of the easement nor can she use a recording statute. Moreover she cannot use the shelter rule here either since C was not likely a SBP.

QUESTION TWO

At issue is the likely outcome of P's lawsuit against C.

Part A

At issue is P's claim for breach of contract. When parties convey land it is a two-step process: first the parties enter into a contract for the sale of land and then there is a period of escrow. Following escrow, closing occurs. At closing is where the actually deed is delivered and at that point the deal is finished. P's first claim arises under the land sale contract.

Land Sale contract - Marketable Title

A contract for the sale of land is required to be in a valid writing satisfying the statute of frauds. Here on 2012, P and C executed a written contract to sell the farm to P for $100,000. The contract stated that the seller "shall covenant against encumbrances with no exceptions". This express provision essentially was stating that the land would not be sold with any encumbrances on it. An encumbrance is something that includes easements. In every contract for the sale of land there is the doctrine of marketable title however. This means that upon closing, the land would not have any defects of title in it, including easements. Therefore even though the contract stated that the land would not be sold with any encumbrances on it, this would be implied in the contract. Here at closing the land had an easement on it with the water company as well as B's easement as argued above. Thus at closing two easements existed on the land.

The problem however is that at closing, under the merger doctrine, the land contract merges into the deed and cannot be used to provide relief to a buyer.

Merger

Under the merger doctrine, the contract is said to merge into the deed and the buyer may not use the contract to recover for defects on the property. Here at closing the land sale contract that C and P entered into would be said to merge into the deed. Thus even though the contract was breached at closing, there could be no relief afforded under the terms of the contract. As such, P cannot make a breach of contract claim here.

Conclusion

In total, P's breach of contact claim would fail because the merger doctrine merged the contract into the deed and it can no longer afford relief to P.

Part B

The next issue then is the buyer's ability to recover under the warranty that was contained within the deed. Deeds contain covenants in them that allow for recovery to a buyer. Whether the buyer can recover depends on the type of deed and covenant contained in a deed.

Type of Deed

There are three kinds of deed: general warranty deeds, special warranty deeds, and quitclaim deeds. Quitclaim deeds do not provide any relief under a covenant. General warranty deeds provide relief under several different kinds of covenants. Here the deed that was given to P contained the covenant that stated there would be no encumbrances on the property, except the easement to Water Co. (W). Thus we must examine that covenant.

Covenant Against Encumbrances

The covenant against encumbrances states that at closing, there will be no encumbrances on property. This is breached immediately at closing and is considered a present covenant on the property. Here at the time of closing there were two easements contained within the property. Since both were on the property, they are both subject to the covenant against encumbrances.

B's Easement

As stated above B has a valid easement on the farm that P bought. Thus this easement will exist on the property and therefore at closing the deed covenant against encumbrances was breached. As such P has a valid cause of action against C for breaching this covenant with respects to B's easement. It does not matter that P saw B's using the road at the time of contract formation; notice is not material for purposes of the covenants. C specifically included a covenant against encumbrances in her deed. Therefore the presence of this one breached that covenant.

W's Easement

As explained above, an easement can be created by express deed. Here in 2013, C deeded an easement to W for water lines along the property. This was during the escrow period. Given that an express easement was likely created via deed to W, W had an easement on the property at closing. The covenant however specifically disclaimed liability for W's easement. Given that C specifically disclaimed the easement in her covenant, and P accepted closing at that time, P likely waived any argument she has that C breached this covenant.

Insofar as this was a present covenant the statute of limitations for it began to run at the time of closing. Therefore P should have raised any objection to this encumbrance at the time that it existed. However P went through with closing, specifically accepting the deed that contained a waiver with W's easement on it. Therefore P cannot likely recover for W's easement under the covenant in the deed.

P can attempt to argue for fraud or some other kind of defense to C's actions here but it is unlikely that such an argument would prevail. It does seem unfair that C would include in the contract a provision stating that there would be no encumbrances in the title, yet during escrow she actually put another on her property. But C specifically included a waiver of this encumbrance in the warranty in her deed. Therefore P would be charged with reading the warranty and seeing such waiver. If P did not like the waiver she should have raised the issue during closing and not accepted the deed as is. Therefore P likely waived any argument against W's easement given her acceptance of the deed with the waiver on it.

Remedies

Typically the remedy for a defect in title to land such as occurred here with B's easement is the difference of the value of the land with the easement on it and the value of the land without the easement on it. Here the difference in value of the land would be $5,000 as the facts indicate that the farm is worth $5,000 less with B's easement on it. Thus P can likely recover $5,000 from C for B's easement in violation of the covenant in her deed.

However P cannot recover the $10,000 that W's encumbrance decreases the value of the land by since the covenant would not extend to that encumbrance as P likely waived it as stated above.

Conclusion

In total, P can recover under the covenant in the warranty deed for B's easement only and she would likely get only $5,000.

Overall Conclusion

P's cause of action against C for breach of contract would fail under the merger doctrine. Yet P can recover under her deed against C for B's easement on the property, but not W's easement.

QUESTION 2: SELECTED ANSWER B

1. Ben v. Polly

Easements

An easement is a right in land granted to a third party. Easement may be created expressly or impliedly. Implied easements may be created by prescription, by prior use, or by necessity. Easements can additionally be classified as appurtenant or in gross. Easements in gross have no dominant estate and are personal in nature and are generally non-transferable.

Appurtenant easements are those which burden one estate (servient estate) while also benefiting another estate (the dominant estate). Appurtenant easements run with the land to subsequent takers who take with notice of the easement. Notice can be actual, constructive, or inquiry. Actual notice arises when the subsequent taker is actually aware of the easement. Constructive notice arises when the easement has been properly recorded. When an easement has been properly recorded, takers are put on constructive notice of the existence of the easement whether or not they were actually aware of the easement. Lastly, inquiry notice arises when based on the facts or circumstances of the property a reasonable person would have inquired about the existence of any easements or interests in land.

Express Easement

An express easement must be in writing.

Here, in 1990, Al deeded an easement for a road along the north side of his farm to his neighbor Ben. The facts indicate that Al deeded the easement to Ben thus satisfying the writing requirement and establishing an express easement. Further, the easement will be classified as an appurtenant easement because Al and Ben are neighbors and therefore the easement concerns the land and benefits Ben's land by allowing an access road, while burdening Ben's land by granting access to a third party.

Additionally, the facts indicate that the easement decreased the fair market value of Al's land by $5,000 which further shows that the easement burdened the farm (the servient estate) thus establishing an easement appurtenant. Because the easement granted to Ben was an easement appurtenant, it will run with the land to successive takers who take with notice of the land.

Priority

Here, because Al deeded the property to Carol who recorded her deed prior to Ben's recording of his easement, it must be determined who has priority. There are three methods of recording statutes in the different jurisdictions: race, race-notice, and notice. If the recording statute applied in the jurisdiction does not apply, the courts will resort to the common law principles of first in time to determine priority. Under the shelter rule, a subsequent purchaser in land may take shelter and be protected under a recording statute, if a previous transferee of land would have otherwise been protected by a recording statute.

Race

Under a race notice jurisdiction, priority goes to the first to record. Here, Carol recorded her deed in 2009 and Ben did not record his deed until 2011. Therefore, between Ben and Carol, in a race jurisdiction, Carol would have priority over Ben. Polly would then be able to use the shelter rule, if it applies, to be protected by Carol's priority under the recording statute and thus Polly would have superior title to Ben. However, if the shelter rule does not apply between Polly and Ben, because Ben recorded his deed in 2011 and Polly did not record her deed until 2014, Ben would take priority and Polly would be burdened by the easement.

Notice

Under a notice recording statute, priority is given to subsequent bona fide purchasers who took property without notice. Notice may be actual, constructive, or inquiry. Actual notice arises when the taker actually knew of the interest. An individual is deemed to have constructive notice when a look into the grantor-grantee index would have put them on notice of the interest. Lastly, inquiry notice arises when the facts or circumstances would have led a reasonable person to inquire about other interests in the land.

Under a notice statute, Polly would have priority over Ben if she could establish that she took the property without notice of Ben's interest. Ben, however, will successfully argue that Polly had notice of his easement both under constructive notice and under inquiry notice. Because Ben recorded his easement in 2011, had Polly looked at the grantor-grantee index for the parcel of land, she would've seen Ben's easements. Further, because Polly had observed Ben traveling on the road, she likely was put on inquiry notice to inquire into Paul's right to be on the land at issue. Further, because Al deeded the farm to Carol and there is no evidence that she paid any value for the farm, she is not a bona fide purchaser protected by the recording statute and Polly could not use the shelter rule in a notice jurisdiction.

Race-Notice

Under a race-notice recording statute, priority is given to the first bona fide purchaser to record without notice. Here, Carol recorded her deed in 2009, Paul subsequently recorded his deed in 2011, and Polly lastly recorded her deed in 2014. Because Carol likely is not a bona fide purchaser since she did not pay value for the farm, priority would go to the next bona fide purchaser who records without notice. However, because Carol has recorded her interest, Polly will argue that Ben was put on notice of the conveyance to Carol. However, because Ben received the deed in 1990 there was likely no requirement for him to look into the grantor-grantee index after he received the easement. However, if so, he will be deemed to have been put on notice. Further, Polly cannot claim priority over Ben because, as discussed above, she also took with notice to the property; thus in a race-notice jurisdiction, the priority will resort to common law rules of first in time and Ben will have priority over Polly.

Therefore, it will likely be determined in any of the three jurisdictions that Ben had priority over Polly and thus Ben will be successful in his action against Polly.

<u>Easement by Prescription</u>

Alternatively, Ben can claim that he acquired an easement by prescription. An easement by prescription requires the holder to take actually, openly, and continuously use the land in a manner hostile to the true owner, for the statutory period. At common law the statutory period for adverse possession was 20 years. Thus, Ben will argue that because he used the land continuously and openly from 1990 to present day, he has acquired an easement by prescription. However, because Ben used the road with permission by Al, his use will not be hostile and he will not succeed on such a claim.

2a. Polly v. Carol (Breach of Contract)

Here, Polly has commenced an action against Carol seeking damages for breach of contract based on the clause in Carol and Polly's written contract stating that "Seller shall covenant against encumbrances with no exceptions." Polly's claim for such a breach may lie wither in the concept of marketable title or a breach of an express condition of the contract.

Implied in any sale of land is a warranty that at closing the seller will convey marketable title. Marketable title warrants that there are no encumbrances on the property which are defined as any interest in a third party that diminishes the value or use of the land but is consistent with a granting of a fee interest in the property. While a seller must convey marketable title at closing, once a deed to the property is delivered and accepted the land sale contract merges with the deed and any rights to sue under the contract are extinguished and the buyer may only sue upon the deed.

Here, Polly has commenced an action against Carol seeking damages for the breach of the clause in the contract covenanting against encumbrances. Polly's claim may arise out of a claim that title was not marketable based on the easement to Ben or the easement to Water Co., or breach of the specific covenant in the agreement. While the easements to Ben and Water Co. are encumbrances which would warrant a breach of the contract or of marketable title, provided that Polly was unaware of them at the time of signing, because the facts indicate that in 2014 Carol executed and delivered to Polly a warranty deed which Polly accepted, the land sale contract has merged with the deed and Polly can no longer sue on the contract and must sue on the deed. Polly may, however, have a claim under the deed which is discussed below.

2b. Polly v. Carol (Breach of Covenant Under the Warranty Deed)

Type of Deed

Upon the transfer of land, the seller may execute and deliver to the buyer one of the following three types of deeds: general warranty deed, a special warranty deed, or a quitclaim deed. The parties' rights under the deed depend on the type of deed granted to the seller. A quitclaim deed contains no covenants or promises to the buyer and is essentially an "as is" deed leaving the buyer with no rights to sue the seller. Alternatively, warranty deeds may include all or any of the six covenants of title including: the covenant of seisin, the right to convey, the covenant against encumbrances, general warranty, further assurances, and quiet enjoyment. Warranty deeds can be classified as either general warranty deeds or special warranty deeds. General warranty deeds are the most protective deed and warrant that neither the seller, or anyone in the chain of title, has breached the covenants included in the deed. Alternatively, a special warranty deed only warrants that the seller has not breached the covenants of title.

Here, Polly is commencing an action for breach of the covenant under the warranty deed. The facts indicate that the deed was a warranty deed containing only the covenant against encumbrances. Because the covenant was included in the deed, Polly may properly sue Carol for breach of the warranty.

Covenant Against Encumbrances

The covenant against encumbrances in a deed warrants that there are no unknown encumbrances on the property. Under title, encumbrances are defined as any right in a third party that diminishes the value or interferes with the use and enjoyment of the land. Such encumbrances include mortgages, liens, easements, and covenants. Here, Polly is suing for breach of the covenant against encumbrances. There are two possible easements on the property which may be the subject of her claim, the easement to Water Co. and the easement to Ben. Because the deed expressly warrants against any encumbrances other than the easement to Water Co., Polly cannot successfully claim a breach of the covenant in relation to that covenant because it was expressly excluded in the deed. However, Polly may be able to assert a breach based on the encumbrance to Ben. The determination of whether Ben's easement is valid is discussed above and, provided it is valid, Carol will likely argue that Polly was put on notice of such easement based on inquiry notice because the facts indicate that she had observed Ben traveling on the road along the north side, but said nothing. Polly will argue that those circumstances alone did not give rise to suspicion that he claimed an interest in the property; however, considering she was aware of his passing over the land, it is reasonable to assume that a buyer would have inquired into the circumstances. Further, Carol will argue that even if she did not have inquiry notice of Ben's interest, she would have constructive interest of Ben's interest because he recorded his deed in the easement in 2011 before Carol and Polly had entered into the land sale contract. Therefore, while Polly can properly claim a breach of the covenant based on the warranty deed received by Carol, provided it is valid, it will likely be determined that she had sufficient notice of the easement.

QUESTION 3

Dirt, a large excavating company, recently replaced all of its gas-powered equipment with more efficient diesel-powered equipment. It placed the old gas-powered equipment in storage until it could sell it.

On May 1, Builder, a general contractor for a large office development, and Dirt signed a valid written contract under which Dirt agreed to perform all the site preparation work for a fee of $1,500,000. Dirt estimated its total cost for the job at $1,300,000. The contract states: "Dirt hereby agrees to commence site work on or before June 1 and to complete all site work on or before September 1." Because no other work could begin until completion of the site preparation, Builder was anxious to avoid delays. To ensure that Dirt would give the job top priority, the contract also states: "Dirt agrees to have all of its equipment available as needed to perform this contract and shall refrain from undertaking all other jobs for the duration of the contract."

On May 29, an unusual high pressure weather system settled over the state.

As a result, on May 30, in an effort to reduce air pollution, the state banned use of all diesel-powered equipment.

On June 2, Dirt told Builder about the ban and stated that it had no way of knowing when it would be lifted. Builder told Dirt to switch to its gas-powered equipment. Dirt replied that using its old gas-powered equipment would add $500,000 to its costs and asked Builder to pay the increased expense. Builder refused.

On June 4, seeing that no site work had begun, Builder emailed Dirt stating that their contract was "terminated."

On June 8, Builder hired another excavating company, which performed the work for $1,800,000.

Dirt has sued Builder for terminating the contract. Builder has countersued Dirt for the $300,000 difference between the original contract price and what it paid the new contractor.

1. Is Dirt likely to prevail in its suit? Discuss.

2. Is Builder likely to prevail in its countersuit? Discuss.

QUESTION 3: SELECTED ANSWER A

Governing Law

The contract involves excavation related to the construction of a large office development. Common law principles, rather than the UCC, will apply as the sale of goods is not implicated.

Dirt's Suit Against Builder for Termination of Contract

Builder's termination of the contract will be wrongful unless one of the relevant grounds for rescission is satisfied. Builder can argue, alternatively, that: 1) Dirt's breach was material; 2) Dirt's comment regarding costs constituted an anticipatory repudiation; 3) Frustration of purpose, or impossibility, gave provided grounds to discharge the K.

Minor versus Material Breach

Breaches of the promises or covenants contained in a contract provide grounds for the non-breaching party to sue for damages. The ability to treat the contract as discharged on the grounds of a breach, however, depends on the nature and extent of the breach itself. A material breach *does* provide the non-breaching party with grounds to discharge the contract. A minor (non-material) breach does not. Whether a breach is material or minor depends on a determination as to whether the non-breaching party received the "benefit of the bargain" sought under the contract. Courts will address an assortment of factors in seeking to arrive at such a determination, including the hardship to the defendant, the reason for the breach, whether the breach was willful or inadvertent, the cost of remedying the breach, the ability of damages to remedy the breach, and the overall degree of completion at the time of the breach.

If a promise or covenant is *implied* into a contract, courts will generally accept substantial performance (as to avoid a breach). If a promise or covenant is *express* in the contract, generally literal compliance is required. However, even when dates are included in a contract, including construction contracts, courts do not construe time to be of the essence *unless otherwise clearly stated.*

Was Time of the Essence

Here, the contract itself reads "Dirt hereby agrees to commence site work on or before June 1 and to complete all site work on or before September 1." It additionally contains a promise from Dirt to have all equipment ready and to refrain from undertaking other jobs during the duration of the contract. Each party will seek to argue in the affirmative/contrary that time is/is not of the essence. Builder will argue that multiple contractual provisions outlining the importance of expediency and availability of supplies mandate a finding that time is of the essence in the contract. However, Dirt can argue that time of the essence was never explicitly stated in the contract, and that any such reading of such a promise would be implied only. Dirt will additionally argue that, if time is not of the essence, then not having started by June 4 -- three days after the intended start date -- would not constitute a material breach and thus Builder could not treat the contract as discharged. Builder will argue the opposite -- time was of the essence; three days late was therefore a material breach, and therefore the contract can be discharged.

Conclusion

A court is more likely to find in Dirt's favor based on these facts. Firstly, the contract did not explicitly state time is of the essence, despite multiple references to the timeliness of performance. Secondly, if time was of the essence, it would likely be in regard to the *completion* rather than the *starting* date. Starting three days late would not constitute a material breach; therefore, even if time was deemed of the essence. The conjunctive power of these two arguments likely means Dirt would prevail and would not have deemed to have been in material breach of the contract by failing to start performance by June 4. This would, therefore, make Builder's termination of the contract improper and Dirt would prevail in his suit, subject to the analysis below.

"Having All Equipment Available"

An explicit term of the contract between Dirt and Builder was that Dirt "agrees to have all of its equipment available as needed to perform this contract..." When Dirt and Builder communicated on June 2, Dirt communicated to Builder that using its old gas-powered equipment would cost an additional $500,000 and asked for the increased payment. The parties will contest what was meant by the term of the contract, and whether Dirt breached the term of the contract by not having gas-powered equipment ready. Dirt will contest that "all of its equipment" refers to the equipment its business employs in carrying out excavation contracts, which, at present, is diesel-powered equipment. Builder will argue the equipment provision mandated for Dirt to have any and all necessary equipment ready to perform.

Builder *likely* has the stronger argument on these facts. Builder can likely demonstrate that the failure to have the necessary equipment to perform the excavation -- the very purpose for which Dirt was hired -- is a material breach of the contract. It is material, Builder will assert, because it deprives Builder of the entirety of the benefit of its bargain; without proper equipment, the contract cannot even begin to be performed. Therefore, as a material breach, Builder has grounds to terminate the contract. Dirt's counter-argument that it had the *reasonably foreseeable necessary* equipment to begin likely won't succeed -- Dirt did still have gas-powered equipment, although it was in storage; when Builder contracted with Dirt, it could expect that Dirt would employ all equipment that it owned in performing the contract. Therefore, Builder likely has a stronger argument that by not having gas-powered equipment ready Dirt was not able to meet the requirement of the contract to have "all of its equipment available as needed to perform this contract." Such a material breach would give proper grounds to terminate the contract on Builder's part, but Builder's argument is by no means a clear and certain winner.

Anticipatory Repudiation Versus Perspective Inability to Perform
An anticipatory repudiation occurs when one party, in a fully bilateral executory contract, communicates explicitly and unequivocally that it will not be able to perform its duties or obligations under the contract. An anticipatory repudiation discharges the non-repudiating party's duty to perform and that party can 1) treat the contract as discharged

2) sue immediately, 3) wait and sue on the contract date, 4) attempt to urge performance by the other party. A perspective inability to perform is a statement by one party to the other expressing doubts or reservations about a potential ability to perform an obligation or duty under the contract. It differs from an anticipatory repudiation in its explicitness and unambiguousness.

Here, Dirt told Builder that using its old gas-powered equipment would add $500,000 to its costs and asked Builder to pay the increased expense. Builder refused the request. Nothing in Dirt's language would rise to the level of an anticipatory repudiation -- it made no representation that it absolutely could not perform under the contract or that it would not, despite an increased cost. It merely requested a greater sum of money due to the elevated cost of performance. Builder could not justifiably have treated Dirt's comment as an anticipatory repudiation. Dirt's comment may have constituted a prospective inability to perform, but analysis as to whether it did or not is largely superfluous derivative of the fact that, even if it was, Builder's duties under the contract would only have been suspended. Builder could not treat the contract as discharged via a perspective inability to perform.

Concluding, Builder could not treat the contract as discharged on grounds of an anticipatory repudiation or perspective inability to perform based on Dirt's comments regarding the increased cost of performance.

Frustration of Purpose
Builder can seek to advance the argument that frustration of purpose provided grounds to discharge its contract with Dirt. Frustration of purpose occurs when a supervening event, which was unforeseeable to the parties, and which neither party expressly assumed the risk of, frustrates the purpose of the contract (i.e., deprives the contract of value and benefit.) Builder will seek to argue that the state's banning of diesel-powered equipment frustrated the purpose of its contract with Dirt, as state regulation due to the unusual weather system was unforeseeable, and that the value and purpose of the contract have been frustrated via this unforeseeable event. Builder will seek to argue

neither party assumed the risk, and the change was not foreseeable to the parties at the time the contract was entered into.

Dirt will likely have a winning counter-argument to Builder's claim of frustration of purpose. While the state regulation has changed the cost of the contract -- and has changed the cost of the contract *to Dirt alone* -- the underlying value and benefit of the contract has remained. The purpose for which the parties contracted is still achievable, and increased cost alone does not frustrate the entire purpose of a construction contract.

A court is more likely to favor Dirt's argument, especially because Builder, in seeking to advance an argument of frustration of purpose, is not in fact the party enduring hardship in this contract from increased cost. While the cost of performance has changed via the state regulation, the basic purpose and value of the contract remains -- the land can be excavated for the purpose of constructing a building subsequently.

Impossibility

Builder could seek to argue, ultimately unsuccessfully, that impossibility and impracticability should allow the contract to be terminated. Impossibility refers to the situation where a subsequent event, which was unforeseeable, which undermined a material element of the contract (or a basic assumption upon which it was formed), and which neither party assumed the risk of, has rendered performance of the contract (by one or both parties) illegal. One form of impossibility is illegality, occurring where the subject matter of the contract has subsequently become illegal after the contract was entered into.

Builder's arguments are likely to fail because, despite the intervening illegality of the use of diesel-powered equipment, the contract itself, and the purpose for which it was formed, has not been rendered illegal. A required-by-law change in the instrumentality used to carry out the contract would not render the contract itself dischargeable on grounds of impossibility. Impossibility would therefore not serve as a viable grounds for discharge of the contract on the part of Builder.

Damages

If Dirt successfully prevails in its suit against Builder on the grounds that Builder impermissibly breached the contract, Dirt can recover its lost profits under the contract. As a general rule in construction contracts, Builder can recover lost profits if the owner breaches prior to commencement of the construction; if the owner breaches during construction, the builder can recover the contract price - the cost of completion. Here, Dirt would receive lost profits -- that is the $1,500,000 - $1,300,000 = $200,000.

Overall Conclusion

Builder's strongest argument to justify terminating the contract was that Dirt's breach of the material term of the contract to have all equipment available needed to perform the contract constituted a material breach by Dirt, and therefore provided grounds for discharge. This is not a clear-cut certainty, however. Impossibility, impracticability, frustration of purpose, and breach of the time for performance clause all would not be winning arguments to justify termination of the contract *for Builder*. However, even if Builder can show Dirt was in material breach of the contract, Dirt likely has some persuasive counter-arguments to avoid liability, found below.

Builder's Countersuit

Much of the analysis regarding potential avenues for Builder to seek to have the contract discharged (rescission) apply to excuse Dirt's performance under the contract. Frustration of purpose, impossibility, and impracticability all provide grounds by which a party's performance under a contract is excused, in addition to providing potential grounds by which a contract can be discharged between the parties. However, as we established above, the contract was likely rightfully discharged because Dirt breached a material term regarding having "all supplies available." That being said, if Dirt's performance was *excused* for a valid reason, Dirt will not be held liable for damages (amount discussed below) under the contract.

Impracticability

Dirt likely has a strong argument for impracticability. Impracticability encompasses the situation where a subsequent event, which was unforeseeable, and has a material effect on an element of the contract or a basic assumption upon which the contract was formed, and which neither party assumed the risk of, has rendered one party's performance extremely or unreasonably difficult or expensive. Here, Dirt will argue that the subsequent enactment of law was unforeseeable because it was the result of an unusual weather system, and that it was inherently unforeseeable. Furthermore, it has had a material effect on the contract (Dirt's cost of performance), and neither party expressly assumed the risk of the event. Builder can counter that Dirt assumed the risk of increased cost of performance via restrictions on the use of certain types of machines by law, but Builder's argument is not overly persuasive. Rather, the cost of increase in Dirt's performance will likely be determinative in the eyes of the court.

The subsequent enactment of new law has increased the cost of Dirt's performance by $500,000, out of an initial cost of $1,300,000 -- a cost increase of less than 50%. Courts, historically, have generally been unwilling to excuse performance under a contract due to the increased cost in performance unless such an increase is excessive and extreme. Here, a less than 50% increase in cost may not meet that standard; although the increase does make the performance on the contract a profit-negative transaction for Dirt, the increase in cost may not be so unreasonable as to excuse performance, a court may find. Nevertheless, Dirt can and should advance the argument -- likely, however, it will be a losing one.

Impossibility

As discussed in detail above, impossibility -- via illegality -- will not serve as a valid excuse to Dirt's performance because the contract itself did not become illegal, rather merely one means by which the contract could be performed became illegal. A court is unlikely to extend the reasoning so far as to entirely excuse Dirt's performance because diesel-powered equipment has been subject to regulation, especially considering the fact that Dirt has gas-powered equipment available. Dirt's arguments will fail on impossibility grounds.

Frustration of Purpose

Dirt's arguments regarding frustration of purpose will similarly fail for the reasons outlined above -- the value, benefit, and purpose of the contract remains despite an increased cost to Dirt. The essence of the contract and its purpose was the excavation, not what type of machine Dirt used in the process. Dirt's arguments will fail on frustration of purpose grounds.

Mutual Mistake

Dirt could seek to argue that his performance is excused via mutual mistake. Mutual mistake applies when both parties are mistaken as to a basic assumption, material to the contract, upon which the contract was formed. Here, Dirt would argue mutual mistake occurred in regards to "equipment available." Dirt could seek to argue there is ambiguity in the term, as Dirt meant diesel-powered equipment while Builder expected the use of all of Dirt's equipment. Dirt's argument will likely not fail -- the term is plain on its face -- "all of its equipment" -- and would be interpreted to require of Dirt to employ all the equipment it owns, which includes gas-powered equipment. While Dirt may have intended a different meaning for the term, because the term is plain on its face and there was not an actual "mistake" regarding the meaning of the term, Dirt's argument will fail. Dirt's subjective belief will not constitute a mutual "mistake" in the eyes of the court.

Damages

An owner's countersuit in a construction contract which has not been fully performed by the breaching party can recover damages in the amount of the difference between the contract price (with the breaching party) and the cost of completion (obtained via the hiring of a third party.) Here, that would provide Builder with the $300,000 damages outlined as the amount of its lawsuit.

Conclusion

If Builder succeeds in showing that failure to have all equipment available was a material breach by Dirt, it can rightfully treat the contract as discharged. Furthermore, it can recover damages from Dirt *if* a court determines that the difficult to Dirt did not rise to the level of impracticability (the most likely finding). Alternatively, if no grounds existed to discharge the contract because the court does not find Dirt has breached a material term, then Dirt can recover the profits it would be entitled to from the contract. If the contract was rightfully discharged but Dirt's performance *did* rise to the level of impracticability, then Dirt would not be paid to force damages. Builder prevailing in regard to both breach and damages is the most likely outcome.

QUESTION 3: SELECTED ANSWER B

Introduction

Applicable law

The issue is whether the UCC applies. The UCC applies to the sale of goods. Goods are things movable and identifiable at the time of contracting. Here, the contract is for the performance of construction services. Construction services are not goods. Therefore, the UCC does not apply. Therefore, the common law governs.

1. Is Dirt likely to prevail in its suit?

Anticipatory repudiation by Builder

The issue is whether Builder anticipatorily repudiated the contract. Anticipatory repudiation occurs when one party unambiguously and clearly states that it will not perform the contract. An anticipatory repudiation counts as a breach. The non-breaching party can either find someone else to do the performance, sue the breaching party, or do nothing. Anticipatory repudiation generally applies to executory contracts. In the event that the contract is wholly executory, then the non-repudiating party can immediately sue for damages, regardless of the date of performance. If the non-breaching party has already performed, then it cannot sue until the time for the other party's performance is due. For anticipatory repudiation in construction contracts before anything has begun, the general measure of damages is the non-breaching party's expected lost profits.

Here, the parties made a valid contract on May 1st. The contract provided that construction would begin on June 1 and that performance was due on September 1. On June 4, Builder stated that the contract was terminated. Saying that a contract is terminated is an anticipatory repudiation--is unambiguous and clear. Builder had no intention of following through on the contract at that point. Moreover, the contract was still executory. Dirt had not commenced any sort of performance, and Builder had not paid anything. As a result, Dirt would have the option of suing for breach of contract at the time of breach. Because the contract was completely executory, Dirt would be entitled to its lost expected profits. In this case, the total fee was expected to be $1,500,000 and the expected cost was $1,300,000. As a result, the expected profits would be $200,000. Thus, Dirt would be likely to win $200,000 if there are no applicable defenses to enforcement.

Mitigating damages-defense

In order for a party to recover damages, they must be certain, causally related to the breach, foreseeable, and unavoidable. Here, the damages are foreseeable and caused by Builder's breach. Had Builder not breached, Dirt would have been paid, and non-payment is a foreseeable consequence of breach. Moreover, the damages here are certain--$200,000. We generally use expectation damages in contract law, which puts the party in as good of a position as they would have been had the contract been performed. Generally, the non-breaching party is required to mitigate damages, which means that they must try to reduce damages as much as possible. In the context of construction contracts that are anticipatorily repudiated, mitigating damages might involve taking other work during the time in which the party was expecting to work for the breaching party. Thus, Builder might claim that Dirt has failed to mitigate damages. However, the fact that Builder made Dirt refrain from entering into any other contracts during this time might hurt the mitigation argument -- Dirt would probably be able to show that it was unable to mitigate due to this clause in the contract. Had the clause not been present, perhaps Dirt would have been out finding other business.

Anticipatory Repudiation by Dirt-defense

The issue is whether Builder might be able to defend on the basis that Dirt actually repudiated first. However, this argument is likely to fail. On June 2, Dirt merely told Builder about the ban and asked Builder to shoulder the increased expenses, after which Builder declined. However, this is not sufficiently unambiguous to constitute an anticipatory repudiation. If a party is uneasy about whether the other party can perform (due to an ambiguous situation like we have here), then the party can demand further assurances from the other party, and may temporarily suspend performance for a commercially reasonable time until it receives those assurances. Here, Dirt did not actually say that it was not going to be able to perform. Had Dirt been unambiguous, then perhaps Builder could have deemed it an anticipatory repudiation and hired another party (one of the options when there is an anticipatory repudiation). However, the June 2 conversation was not clear enough. It is perfectly possible that Dirt may perform the contract regardless. Therefore, this defense would be unlikely to be effective.

Breach of Promise/Condition by Dirt-defense

The issue is whether Dirt breached a condition of the contract such that Builder's obligation to perform was discharged. A promise is something that a party is supposed to do under a contract. A condition is an event that, if it does not occur, means the entire contract does not come into effect. Courts generally construe terms as promises as opposed to conditions, because they do not want an entire forfeiture of the contract.

Builder may argue that the June 1 start date was a condition precedent to the contract taking effect. Essentially, they would say that, because Dirt had yet to commence construction by June 1 (indeed, even by June 4), that the condition was not satisfied and the contract did not take effect. However, a court would probably not buy this argument. There are two types of conditions--express and implied. An express condition must be in the contract explicitly in conditional language ("on condition that"), which was not present here. An implied condition may arise from the intent of the parties. Here, Builder was worried about timing, but there is insufficient evidence to infer that the start date was a condition to Builder's entire performance. Thus, a court would likely construe the start date as a mere promise. Indeed, the courts abhor a forfeiture.

In the event that the start date is considered a promise, then the common law doctrine of substantial performance applies. Substantial performance holds that a non-breaching party has a duty to perform if the breaching party has still substantially performed her end of the bargain. There must be a "material breach" in order for the non-breaching party to be completely discharged. When determining whether there has been substantial performance, the courts take into account (i) prejudice to breaching party; (ii) prejudice to breaching party; (iii) amount of performance rendered; (iv) whether the breach was willful; (v) cost of fixing the problem; and (vi) a variety of similar factors.

In service contracts, time for completion is generally not considered a material breach if performance is completed slightly late. The only time when a complete breach and forfeiture might be found is when there is a "time of the essence" clause, which must be very explicit. There was no such clause in this contract, and the breach only applied to the *start* of performance, so it would be very unlikely for a court to find that Dirt materially breached to the extent that Builder will be completely discharged form performance.

Conclusion

Overall, it appears that Dirt would have a good case against Builder for breach of contract for the amount of $200,000.

Is Builder likely to prevail in its countersuit?

Anticipatory repudiation by Dirt

This is the same argument as has been described above. Essentially, Dirt's statements over the course of the June 4 conversation are unlikely to constitute a full-blown anticipatory repudiation. Builder should have first demanded further assurances before terminating the contract and hiring someone else.

Breach of promise/condition by Dirt

This is the same argument as has been described above. Essentially, it is unlikely that a court would find the start date to be a condition precedent to effectiveness of the contract. Moreover, it is unlikely that Dirt's failure to start completely on time would count as a material breach justifying Builder's non-performance.

Impossibility-defense

Dirt might argue in defense that it would be unable to perform its end of the contract due to supervening impossibility. Indeed, in many cases, a subsequent law or regulation may render a party's performance illegal or impossible. In such case, that party may be excused from performing. Generally, the party claiming excuse must have not expressly borne the risk.

Here, the government banned all diesel-powered equipment two days before Dirt was supposed to commence performance. This was certainly unexpected, and was the result of the May 29 high-pressure weather system. However, performance is definitely not impossible. Dirt still has its gas-powered equipment, which it could use to complete the project. It might be more expensive to do so, but mere increase in expense is insufficient for an impossibility defense. Therefore, impossibility would not be an effective defense.

Impracticability-defense

Dirt might argue in defense that it should be excused from performance due to supervening impracticability. Impracticability is a defense where the occurrence of an unforeseeable event happens, which renders performance impracticable. The unforeseeable event must affect an underlying assumption of the agreement. The party claiming excuse must not have borne the risk. Generally, the mere inability to make a profit is not sufficient for a claim of impracticability.

Here, the high pressure system was characterized as unusual. Builder might argue that strange weather systems are foreseeable, and that Dirt should have known that this was a possibility. On the other hand, Dirt would claim that a weather system resulting in the banning of all diesel-powered equipment is not foreseeable at all. Overall, it would probably be seen as unforeseeable. Moreover, the ban had an effect on an underlying assumption of the contract. Dirt was expecting to use its diesel equipment--it had put all of its old equipment in storage. Moreover, if Dirt knew that it would have to spend an additional $500,000, it would not have accepted a $1,500,000 contract price. There is no evidence that either party expressly assumed the risk (though sellers generally bear the risk in sale of goods contracts, and a court could, by analogy, deem that Dirt was allocated the risk). The key question is whether the ban makes performance impracticable. Dirt is a large excavation company, which presumably has a lot of contracts. If Dirt had to use its gas equipment, it would expect to see a $300,000 loss on this job. It is unclear the effect that such a loss would have on Dirt, but a court would probably find that such a loss is insufficient to make performance of the contract wholly impracticable. It is possible that a court could find that performance is impracticable, but it is rather unlikely.

Mistake-defense

Dirt might try to argue that there was a mutual mistake, which should lead to discharge of contractual duties. Mutual mistake occurs when both parties were mistaken about a fundamental aspect of the contract. Dirt could argue that both parties mistakenly assumed that Dirt would be able to use its diesel-powered machines. The fact that a basic assumption has been violated (by Dirt having to use gas-powered equipment) could perhaps render the contract unenforceable and both parties would be excused. This is somewhat of a stretch of an argument. It depends on whether Builder actually had diesel as a basic assumption of the contract, and whether either side assumed the risk.

Damages

$300,000 would be the proper expectation damages. Builder would get the difference between the contract price and the reasonable cover price.

Conclusion

For the reasons mentioned, Builder would be unlikely to win its countersuit.

QUESTION 4

State X has a valid contract with public school teachers providing a fixed salary schedule. State X recently passed legislation to address its failing public schools. Now, when a school falls below established standards, each teacher at that school has 10% of his or her salary withheld each pay period for a maximum of two years. The withholding ends, and the money is returned with interest, upon the completion of a ten-hour certification program or termination of employment.

City High is a public school in State X where salary withholding has begun.

Bob has been a teacher at City High for the past three years. Paige is a highly-regarded probationary teacher at City High. A probationary teacher may be terminated for any reason upon written notice within the first year of employment.

Bob and Paige have been outspoken opponents of the State X law and its application to City High, appearing at various community and school board meetings throughout the school year.

Shortly before the end of Paige's first year of employment, City High served her with written notice terminating employment, and refunded the money withheld with interest.

Bob and Paige have sued State X, the Attorney General of State X, and City High in federal court seeking damages and injunctive relief. State X and the Attorney General have moved to dismiss the suit based on standing and the Eleventh Amendment.

1.   Did City High's termination of Paige without a hearing violate the procedural due process guaranty of the Fourteenth Amendment to the United States Constitution? Discuss.

2.   How should the court rule on the State and the Attorney General's motion? Discuss.

QUESTION 4: SELECTED ANSWER A

1. WHETHER PAIGE'S TERMINATION VIOLATED HER FOURTEENTH AMENDMENT PROCEDURAL DUE PROCESS RIGHTS

The Due Process Clause of the Fourteenth Amendment prohibits the states from depriving any person of life, liberty or property without due process of law. Due process generally requires a fair procedure, usually notice and a hearing. Under procedural due process analysis, the first inquiry is whether the plaintiff had a constitutionally protected liberty or property interest. If the plaintiff has a protected interest, the court will then balance that interest against the state's interests under *Matthews*. The court will also look to the risk of erroneous deprivation and whether additional procedural safeguards would reduce such risk. The issue for Paige (P) is therefore (1) whether she has a protected liberty or property interest, and (2) whether she was entitled to a fairer process.

WHETHER PAIGE HAS A CONSTITUTIONALLY PROTECTED LIBERTY OR PROPERTY INTEREST

Property Interest

The issue is whether P's probationary employment at City High is a protected property interest.   Traditionally, the Supreme Court differentiated between "rights" and "privileges" and provided that only "rights" are protected under the Due Process Clause. The Court since *Goldberg*, however, has held that a property interest is protected by the Due Process Clause if the plaintiff has a "legitimate claim of entitlement."

Under Supreme Court precedent, a tenured public school teacher has a protected property interest in their employment; however, a teacher does not have a protected interest if she is terminable at will during an initial probationary period. *Kelly*. P is a probationary teacher and may be terminated for any reason upon written notice within the first year of employment. There is also no indication that City High made her any assurances that she would not be fired during the probationary period. P, therefore, does not have a legitimate claim of entitlement to her job and thus has no protected property interest.

Liberty Interest

The Court has also recognized that when a person's freedom of movement is restrained (e.g., detention) or when a person's constitutional rights are denied, the person has a liberty interest that is protected by the Due Process Clause. P may argue that she was terminated during her first year, not because of poor performance, but rather in retaliation for her exercising her First Amendment rights in speaking out against the State's law that withholds teachers' salaries based on the school's performance. If P can make a showing that her First Amendment rights were violated, she could trigger due process protections and seek additional termination procedures beyond the written notice provided to her before she was fired.

Some speech is not protected under the First Amendment. Generally, the speech of a public employee made in the course of their employment can be regulated by the government employer. Employees' speech outside the scope of their work and regarding public issues, however, is protected by the First Amendment. P will argue that her outspoken criticism of the State law at community and school board meetings was not related to her job duties and therefore is protected. City High may argue that it was related to the job and therefore not protected. A court will likely find her speech protected.

Content-based regulations of speech must meet strict scrutiny; the restriction must be necessary to achieve a compelling government purpose. Content-neutral restrictions must meet intermediate scrutiny; they must be substantially related to and narrowly tailor to achieve an important government purpose. P would need to show that her termination was in relation for her speech, which would constitute a content-based regulation because it is based on her viewpoint. If P can make this showing, the state would have to meet strict scrutiny, and would likely fail. Regardless, P may be able to show that she had a protected liberty interest in her Free Speech rights under the First Amendment.

MATTHEWS BALANCING TEST

If the court recognizes P's liberty interest, it must apply the *Matthew* balancing test to determine whether she should have been entitled to any additional procedures beyond her pre-termination notice. The court will balance: (1) the private interest affected by the government action, (2) the government's interest including administrative and fiscal burdens, and (3) the risk of erroneous deprivate and the value of additional procedural safeguards.

First, P has a relatively strong private interest in her job. Employment is the way individuals earn money to support themselves. Generally courts have viewed employment interests as quite weighty. Second, the state has an interest in not having to provide a full hearing on this type of probationary termination. The state likely saves a lot of money by not having to develop elaborate procedures to ensure that all of its termination decisions are fair. This interest is therefore quite strong. Finally, P will argue that the risk that she was fired because of her First Amendment rights is high, and that a few additional procedures such as allowing her to present countervailing evidence, or a hearing in front of the school board or committee would allow her to challenge the basis of the decision and force City High to justify their actions, or at least show that the basis of the decision was not to silence her.

The outcome of the *Matthews* test is difficult to predict. However, a court may require City High to provide at least minimal additional protections such as a post-termination hearing.

2. WHETHER THE COURT SHOULD GRANT THE STATE AND ATTORNEY GENERAL'S MOTION TO DISMISS

STANDING

The State and the Attorney General (AG) filed a motion to dismiss for lack of standing and under the Eleventh Amendment. First, standing is the issue of whether the plaintiff is the proper party to bring the claim before a federal court. The plaintiff must have a concrete stake in the outcome of the litigation. The Court has interpreted Article III's conferral of the judicial power over "cases" and "controversies" to require the plaintiff to show (i) that he has suffered an injury in fact (injury in fact), and (ii) that the defendant's conduct was the cause of that injury such that a favorable court decision will remedy the injury (causation and redressability). The issue for Bob (B) and P is therefore whether they can demonstrate injury in fact, causation and redressability.

First, the requirement that the plaintiff prove an injury in fact is generally satisfied if the plaintiff shows that they suffered an injury that was actionable at common law, such as pecuniary loss. However, the Court has also recognized an injury in fact where the plaintiff's constitutional or statutory rights have been violated. Environmental, aesthetic, and stigmatic injuries are also judicially cognizable. However, when a plaintiff is seeking injunctive relief, he must show that there is a concrete, imminent threat of future injury that is neither conjectural nor speculative. *Lyons*.

Here, B and P are challenging the State law seeking damages and injunctive relief. They would argue that they have suffered a pecuniary injury because a portion of their salaries was withheld. This is likely sufficient. City High may argue that because their salaries are refunded with interest if they are terminated or complete a certificate program, that there is no real financial loss. B and P, however, will probably succeed in arguing that even a temporary pay cut is a sufficient financial injury. The extent of the injury is generally de minimus. With regard to the injunction, B and P will likely succeed in arguing that they are presently suffering from the financial injury and that will continue in the future; therefore it is sufficiently imminent and concrete. In conclusion, the court should likely find that B and P have shown an injury in fact based on the loss of income, even if temporary. P may have an additional basis for standing by arguing that she was terminated based on protected First Amendment activities. Either would likely be sufficient.

Second, causation and redressability are easily met here. B and P can clearly show that lost earnings are directly caused by the pay withholding required by the statute, and that a court order reimbursing them or enjoining enforcement of the statute would remedy this injury. In conclusion, B and P will likely succeed in showing that they have Article III standing, and therefore the court should deny the State and the AG's motion to dismiss.

ELEVENTH AMENDMENT

The State and the AG also seek dismissal of the suit based on the Eleventh Amendment, which provides that a state is immune from suit in federal court. The Eleventh Amendment is similar, if not identical, to the doctrine of state sovereign immunity, which also applies to suits against states in state court. *Alden v. Maine*. A state may waive sovereign immunity under certain conditions, and Congress can override state sovereign immunity by statute using its enforcement powers under Section 5 of the Fourteenth Amendment. In addition, state officers may be sued in their official capacities to enjoin the enforcement of a state law under *Ex Parte Young*. A state officer may also be sued in his or her individual capacity for retroactive damages, and may be indemnified by the state. So the question depends on the party being sued and the basis of the claim.

The State may not be sued in federal court under the Eleventh Amendment. The court will therefore dismiss B and P's claims against the state. The AG, however, may be sued in his individual capacity to enjoin him from enforcing the state law being challenged. If B and P's claims allege that the AG is liable for their financial losses, he may also be sued in his individual capacity for money damages. However, B and P do not appear to have alleged that the AG is personally liable, or liable under a theory of respondeat superior; therefore he is likely not a proper party for the individual damages action.

In conclusion, the court should grant the motion in part. The claims against the State should be dismissed. The claim for injunctive relief should be upheld against the AG, and potentially also the claim for damages if B and P allege that the AG is liable for damages.

QUESTION 4: SELECTED ANSWER B

1. City High's Termination of Paige

14th Amendment--Due Process

The Due Process clause of the 14th Amendment prevents the government from taking a person's life, liberty, or property without first giving them due process of law. The due process clause has been interpreted to have two sets of rights: substantive due process and procedural due process. Substantive due process prevents the government from arbitrarily denying rights. Procedural due process requires notice and a hearing before (or sometimes after) the government takes a person's life, liberty, or property. Here, Paige is claiming that she was deprived of her right to liberty in her freedom of speech and her right to government employment without procedural due process.

In analyzing a procedural due process claim, the court first determines whether a person's life, liberty, or property has been taken from her. Then, the court determines what process, if any, was due before or after the taking of this right. The Supreme Court laid out this analysis in Matthews v. Eldridge. The court balances three factors: (i) the individual's interest in the right at issue, (ii) the government's interest in efficiency, and (iii) the likely added value of additional protective procedures.

Paige's life has not been taken; thus her claim must be that she was deprived of a liberty interest or a property interest.

A person has a liberty interest in being free from being restricted in movement and in being free to engage in constitutional rights. Paige was not restricted in movement, but she may argue that she was restricted from engaging in a 1st Amendment right, the right to free speech. Sometimes the right to free speech intersects with government employment and the right of the government to control its employees. This is the case here because Paige is a government employee, but she also has been engaging in free speech as an outspoken opponent at various community and school board meetings of a State X law that affects teacher pay. Generally, a government employee has a right to free speech on matters not connected with her employment, and any government restriction of this right is subject to strict scrutiny; it will only be upheld if the government action is necessary to achieve a compelling government purpose. This is a very high burden to satisfy and the government will usually lose. Here, Paige was engaged in speech not associated with her employment because she spoke out against a State X law in her individual capacity as a citizen, not as an employee. Thus, a court could find that if her firing was based on her speech (as she was a "highly regarded" probationary teacher) then she was denied her right to liberty without due process. To determine the amount of process that was due, the court will balance the Matthews factors and likely find that she was entitled to a hearing before termination. The right to speech is great and highly regarded in society and a hearing would be likely to remedy the wrongful termination to great process is added. Moreover, the government interest in efficiency would not overcome these other two factors.

Alternatively, Paige will argue that she has a property interest in her employment. For a person to have a property interest, the Supreme Court has explained that the person must have an entitlement to the property. This entitlement must come from something concrete such as a state law. Generally, employment is at will. In other words, either an employee or an employer can terminate a contract at any time without notice and for any reason (except an illegal reason). Such an employee does not have an entitlement to property because there is no promise of future employment. A tenured employee who can only be fired for cause, on the other hand, has an entitlement to continued employment and is entitled to notice and a hearing before her employment is terminated by the government.

Here, Paige was a probationary teacher at City High, a public school. As a probationary teacher, she could be terminated for any reason upon written notice within the first year of employment. While still in this probationary period, City High notified Paige of her termination. City High is a government actor because it is a public school. Thus the only issue is whether Paige had a property interest that could give rise to a right to due process before her termination. A court will likely find that because Paige's employment was essentially at will during the probationary period, she had no right to continued employment. She was not entitled to future employment because as a probationary employee her contract clearly stated that she could be terminated for any reason. Thus, when City High terminated her employment, it did not deny Paige any property interest and no process was due.

If a court were to find that Paige had a property interest in continued employment at City High, then the next step the court would engage in is determining what process is due before the government can lawfully take the person's property.

Here, the individual's interest is great. Employment is an important aspect of a person's life because it is generally a person's greatest (if not their only) source of income. Being deprived of an income can have serious consequences on a person's life as they may be unable to pay their bills, put food on the table, etc. Thus, a person has a strong interest in continued employment. The government too has a strong interest here, though. The government would incur a significant cost by having to hold a hearing every time that it discharges a government employee. This could have a number of negative consequences. For one thing, it may result in ossification in government hiring because the government would be weary of entering into employment contracts if terminating such contracts would require a hearing. It would also place a financial burden on the state as it would have to pay for the procedures necessary for the hearing, which would be due every time the government seeks to fire an employee. Finally, as to the last factor--the value of the added protections to the individual's rights-- a court would likely find this to be relatively little. There are many reasons for which the government may choose to discharge an employee, particularly a probationary employee, and most of these would be legal because employment is presumed at will. Thus, the hearing would probably provide little use, as the government would only need to show that it sought to discontinue the employment relationship.

In conclusion, a court may find that termination of Paige without a hearing violated the procedural due process guarantee of her liberty. However a court is unlikely to find that City High's termination of Paige without a hearing violated the procedural due process guarantee of the 14th Amendment on the grounds of denial of a right to property.

2. State's and Attorney General's motion

The State and the Attorney General have moved to dismiss on standing grounds and the 11th Amendment. Each will be handled in turn.

Standing

A plaintiff must have standing to assert a claim in federal court. Standing is a judicial doctrine developed from interpretation of Article III of the United States Constitution, which requires that courts can only hear "cases and controversies." The Supreme Court has interpreted this to mean that courts cannot give advisory opinions. For a case or controversy to exist, the plaintiff must have an injury in fact, caused by the action which the plaintiff is challenging, and the injury must be capable of being remedied by a judgment in his favor. An injury in fact occurs when a plaintiff has a concrete stake in the litigation that is not generally held by all other people. The injury is typically an economic injury, but need not necessarily be.

Here, Bob has standing because he can show injury in fact, causation and redressability. He is a teacher at a school that withholds 10% of his salary each period. This injury was caused by the State X legislation which Bob is challenging and it will be redressed by a judgment in his favor because such a judgment would rescind the legislation resulting in Bob receiving his full salary.

Paige too has standing. She can show injury in fact because she lost her job so she lost the income stream associated with that job. This job loss was caused by the fact that City High terminated her employment. And this injury can be redressed by an injunction requiring City High to rehire her and damages for her lost wages.

11th Amendment

The 11th Amendment to the United States Constitution has been interpreted by the U.S. Supreme Court to provide state governments with immunity from suit by private citizens or foreign countries suing in federal court. There are a number of exceptions to the 11th Amendment's bar on private individual suits against the State, including when the State waives its sovereign immunity, and when Congress authorizes suit within its 14th Amendment powers. Moreover, even though the 11th Amendment bars federal courts from hearing suits brought by individuals against States, it does not prevent courts from hearing cases brought by individuals against State officers in their individual capacity or in their official capacity. However, the Amendment does bar suits brought against State officers in their official capacity if the suit seeks damages to be paid out of the State's treasury.

Suit Against the State

Here, the suit against State X will be prohibited by the 11th Amendment. This is a suit by private individuals, Bob and Paige, against a State, State X, brought in federal court. As such, it falls within the 11th Amendment's immunity. Moreover, there is no evidence that the State has waived its sovereign immunity. Nor is there any evidence that Congress has abrogated sovereign immunity in accordance with its 14th Amendment powers for cases brought by teachers against the State for termination or withholding of wages. Thus, the case against State X should be dismissed.

Suit Against the Attorney General

Bob and Paige have also named the Attorney General of State X in their suit. Whether this claim will be barred by 11th Amendment sovereign immunity will depend on whether Bob and Paige are suing the Attorney General in his individual capacity or his official capacity. If they are suing him as an individual, the suit, both for injunctive relief and damages, will not be barred and the Attorney General's motion to dismiss will be denied. The reason is that the 11th Amendment does not protect officials from suit in their individual capacity.

If Bob and Paige have sued the Attorney General in his official capacity, the 11th Amendment will have different effects on the suit for an injunction than on the suit for damages. The suit for an injunction will not be dismissed under the 11th Amendment because it does not prevent individuals from suing officials for injunctive relief. The 11th

Amendment will, however, bar the suit if the suit is for damages to be taken out of the State's coffers. Such a suit is barred by the 11th Amendment and the Attorney General's motion to dismiss should therefore be granted.

QUESTION 5

In 2003, while planning their wedding, Harry and Wanda, a California couple, spent weeks discussing how they could each own and control their respective salaries. Sometime before their wedding, they prepared a document in which they stated, "After we marry, Wanda's salary is her property and Harry's salary is his property." At the same time, they prepared a separate document in which they stated, "We agree we do not need legal advice." They signed and dated each document. They subsequently married.

In 2004, Harry used his salary to buy a condominium and took title in his name alone. Harry and Wanda moved into the condominium.

In 2005, Harry and Wanda opened a joint savings account at their local bank. Each year thereafter, they each deposited $5,000 from their salaries into the account.

In 2015, Harry discovered that Wanda used money from their joint account to buy rental property and take title in her name alone.

In 2016, Harry and Wanda permanently separated and Wanda moved out of the condominium. Wanda thereafter required emergency surgery for a medical condition, resulting in a hospital bill of $50,000. Harry later filed a petition for dissolution of marriage.

What are Harry's and Wanda's rights and liabilities, if any, regarding:

1. The condominium? Discuss.

2. The joint savings account? Discuss.

3. The rental property? Discuss.

4. The hospital bill? Discuss.

Answer according to California law.

QUESTION 5: SELECTED ANSWER A

Community Property and Separate Property

California is a community property (CP) state. Property acquired during a valid marriage while domiciled in CA is presumed to be CP. Property acquired before marriage or after permanent separation is presumed to be separate property (SP). Property acquired during marriage through gift, bequest, devise or descent is also presumed to be SP. Under the source rule, tracing will be permitted to determine the source of the funds, and therefore the character of the asset as CP or SP. Upon divorce, CP will be divided equally in kind unless some special rule requires deviation from this equal division, or the spouses agree otherwise in writing or orally in open court.

Prenuptial Agreement

Spouses may deviate from the community property presumption by agreeing that their salaries, for instance, which normally would be a product of community labor during the marriage and thus CP, be SP. They may do so before the marriage through a written prenuptial agreement. Prenuptial agreements must be voluntary and not unconscionable. A court will find a prenup to be unconscionable if the terms are unfair, or if a spouse did not know the extent of the other spouse's property before signing the agreement. Additionally, prenuptial agreements must be in writing. A court will find that a prenup is not voluntarily executed if a spouse is not represented by counsel before signing the agreement. In order to rebut the presumption of involuntariness without counsel, the spouse not represented by counsel must be advised to seek the advice of counsel in writing, and must waive that right in writing, and if she does waive that right, she must be allowed 7 days between the presentation of a prenuptial agreement and the signing of it, and she must also write, in a separate writing, that she understands the rights she is giving up, and from whom she received the information regarding what the extent is of her spouse's property.

Here, while planning their wedding, Henry and Wanda, both California residents, spent "weeks" discussing "how they could each own and control their respective salaries." Although it is not clear how long before the wedding this occurred, merely, "sometime before their wedding," they jointly "prepared a document in which they stated, 'After we marry, Wanda's salary is her property and Harry's salary is his property.'" They both signed and dated this document. Simultaneously, they "prepared a separate document in which they stated, 'We agree we do not need legal advice,'" which was also signed and dated by both of them. After doing so, they married.

Formalities of Prenuptial Agreement Not Followed: Voluntariness and Unconscionability
As discussed above, a prenuptial agreement must be in writing. It appears from the facts that Henry and Wanda were attempting to create a prenuptial agreement through the "document" that they prepared "sometime before their wedding" in which they agreed that Wanda's salary is her "[separate] property" and Harry's salary is his "[separate] property." Although couples may choose to contract around the general CP presumption through a prenuptial agreement, they must do so voluntarily and it must not be unconscionable. Because neither spouse was represented by counsel, the agreement is presumed to be involuntary. As stated above, this presumption can be rebutted if the spouses who are not represented by counsel are advised to seek counsel and explicitly waive that in writing. Here, it appears that the couple attempted to waive this right to counsel by stating, "We agree we do not need legal advice." This may be a sufficient writing in a court's opinion to waive the right to counsel. Nonetheless, there is still a problem with voluntariness, here. Even if this right is waived in a signed writing, the unrepresented couple must still be given 7 days with which to mull over the prenuptial agreement.

Either spouse (depending on the asset discussed below) may argue that because they spent "weeks discussing how they could each own and control their respective salaries," this was more than enough to satisfy the 7 day rule. However, because the agreement was signed simultaneously with their waiver of counsel, and there is nothing in the facts to demonstrate that there was a period of 7 days AFTER presentation of the document and signing, given that the facts only state "sometime before their wedding" they prepared a document. If this document was prepared and signed 2 hours before the wedding, this would not be deemed voluntary, and may even be deemed unconscionable by a court given its unfairness.

Additionally, neither spouse executed an additional separate document stating that they understood the rights that they were giving up and that they stated the source where they got information about the other spouse's financial assets and liabilities. Therefore, this prenuptial agreement will not be deemed voluntary. However, it probably will not be deemed unconscionable because it does not appear that the terms were patently unfair, given that both spouses were attempting to transmute their salaries into SP, and it does not appear that either spouse was hiding substantial debts or liabilities or significant assets from the other spouse.

In sum, this prenuptial agreement is not likely effective. This will mean that the analysis below will reflect the fact that earnings during marriage will remain CP for purposes of the analysis. Nonetheless, I will still discuss the possibility that this agreement is valid within each spouse's argument, and how that may arguably alter the characterization of property, below.

What are Harry's and Wanda's rights and liabilities regarding:

1. The Condominium

Title Presumption

Property titled in one spouse's name alone is *not* presumably SP in CA.

Here, Henry will argue that he took title in the condominium alone, and therefore it is his separate property.

Wanda will argue that this is not conclusive in California, because ownership does not necessarily follow title. Wanda has the stronger argument here. She will argue that the court must trace, using the source rule to determine the character of the condo.

General CP Presumption

Assets acquired during marriage are presumably CP.

Wanda will argue that because the condo was purchased during the marriage, in 2004, it was presumably CP. She will argue that it is irrelevant that the condo was titled in Henry's name alone, because the court can trace.

Tracing: Source Rule

Under the source rule, a court will trace the assets used to purchase a particular property during marriage to determine its character.

Wanda will argue that by tracing, the court will determine that the condo was purchased with Harry's salary during marriage, and therefore it is CP.

Harry will argue that the prenup was valid, in which they agreed that his salary during marriage would be his separate property, and therefore by purchasing the condo with his salary, which is SP, and since SP breeds SP, the condo is also his SP.

Harry's argument will likely fail because, as discussed above, the prenup is likely invalid and therefore the salaries of both spouses earned during marriage will be community property, and therefore by purchasing the condo with CP funds, the condo itself is CP and it is immaterial that it is titled in Henry's name alone.

Transmutation

Spouses may alter the character of property from CP to SP, or from one spouse's SP to the other spouse's SP, or from SP to CP. After the "easy transmutation period" ended, courts now require transmutations to be in writing, and consented to or accepted by the spouse whose property is changing in nature, and the writing must explicitly state that a change in property is occurring.

Harry will argue that a transmutation of the CP condo occurred when he titled it in his sole name. He will argue that this was a gift from the community to his separate property, and that titling it in his own name was sufficient for a transmutation.

Wanda will argue that this was not sufficient for a transmutation because she did not consent to the change of CP to SP and given that she is the adversely affected spouse, her consent or acceptance was required, and that there is also no writing in the title document stating that the property is changing in form from CP to SP. Wanda has the stronger argument here, and the title of the property will not be deemed a transmutation.

Gifts Between Spouses

As a last ditch effort, Harry will argue that the condo was a gift between spouses and therefore was a valid transmutation that did not need to be in writing. An exception to the writing requirement for valid transmutations is when a gift of a personal nature is given from one spouse to another, and that gift is used primarily by the recipient spouse and is not substantial in nature, taking into consideration the financial situation of the couple.

Wanda will argue that a condo is not tangible personal property, and a condo is also substantial in nature, financially, given that they did not come into the marriage with significant amounts of SP, and moreover, the condo was used by both of them because they both "moved into the condominium." Therefore, Harry's argument that the condo was a gift from CP to SP will fail.

Conclusion

The condo is CP because it was purchased with earnings during marriage and the prenup is likely invalid. Therefore, it will be subject to equal division in kind upon divorce and Harry and Wanda will each take 50% of the proceeds from the sale of the house, assuming it is sold.

2. The joint savings account

Jointly Titled Property CP Presumption

In CA, when title to property is taken in joint form, there is a presumption that the character of the property is CP unless in the title document or elsewhere it is stated that a portion or all of the property is to be reserved as an SP ownership interest. In this case, under *Lucas*, a court will not allow tracing to determine the funds used to purchase a jointly titled home through the source rule and the property will be deemed CP. However, this joint presumption does not apply to bank accounts. With bank accounts, a court will allow jointly titled bank accounts to be traced to determine the source of funds and how it should be characterized.

Tracing

Because both spouses deposited $5,000 each from their salaries during the valid marriage in 2005 into the account, and these salaries were earned during marriage, property earned during marriage through community labor during the economic community is CP. In light of the fact that the prenuptial agreement is likely not valid, both spouse's salaries would be CP, and therefore the court would trace to the source of these funds and determine that the bank account is CP. If, for some reason, the court found that the prenup was valid, and therefore each spouse's salary was SP, then the account would be comprised of $5,000 worth of Wanda's SP and $5,000 worth of Harry's SP. However, this is unlikely.

Conclusion

Presuming that the prenup was invalid, the characterization of the joint savings account would be 100% CP, and therefore should be subject to the equal division in kind rule upon divorce, and whatever is left in the account will be divided equally between the spouses.

3. The rental property

Title Presumption

Property titled in one spouse's name alone is *not* presumably SP in CA.

Here, Wanda will argue that she took title in the rental property alone, and therefore it is her separate property.

Harry will argue that this is not conclusive in California, because ownership does not necessarily follow title. Henry has the stronger argument here. He will argue that the court must trace, using the source rule to determine the character of the rental property.

General CP Presumption

Assets acquired during marriage are presumably CP.

Harry will argue that because the rental property was purchased during the marriage, in 2015, it was presumably CP. He will argue that it is irrelevant that the rental was titled in Wanda's name alone, because the court can trace.

Tracing: Source Rule

Under the source rule, a court will trace the assets used to purchase a particular property during marriage to determine its character.

Harry will argue that, by tracing, the court will determine that the rental was purchased with both spouses' salaries during marriage, and therefore it is CP. He will argue that because the funds were taken from the joint savings account, which is conclusively CP if the prenup was invalid, therefore Wanda used CP funds to purchase the rental, and therefore since CP breeds CP, the rental property is also CP.

Wanda will unconvincingly argue that the prenup was valid, in stark contrast to her earlier argument, stating that the couple agreed that her salary during marriage would be her separate property, and therefore by purchasing the rental with her salary, which is SP, and since SP breeds SP, the rental is also her SP.

Wanda's argument will likely fail because, as discussed above, the prenup is likely invalid and therefore the salaries of both spouses earned during marriage will be community property, and therefore by purchasing the rental with CP funds held in the bank account, the rental itself is CP and it is immaterial that it is titled in Wanda's name alone.

Transmutation

Spouses may alter the character of property from CP to SP, or from one spouse's SP to the other spouse's SP, or from SP to CP. After the "easy transmutation period" ended, courts now require transmutations to be in writing, and consented to or accepted by the spouse whose property is changing in nature, and the writing must explicitly state that a change in property is occurring.

Wanda will argue that a transmutation of the CP rental occurred when she titled it in her sole name. She will argue that this was a gift from the community to her separate property, and that titling it in her own name was sufficient for a transmutation.

Harry will argue that this was not sufficient for a transmutation because he did not consent to the change of CP to SP and given that he is the adversely affected spouse, his consent or acceptance was required, and that there is also no writing in the title document stating that the property is changing in form from CP to SP. Harry has the stronger argument here, and the title of the property will not be deemed a transmutation.

Gifts Between Spouses

Finally, Wanda will argue that the rental was a gift between spouses and therefore was a valid transmutation that did not need to be in writing. An exception to the writing requirement for valid transmutations is when a gift of a personal nature is given from one spouse to another, and that gift is used primarily by the recipient spouse and is not substantial in nature, taking into consideration the financial situation of the couple.

Harry will argue that a rental property is not tangible personal property, and a rental property is also substantial in nature, financially, given that they did not come into the marriage with significant amounts of SP.

Wanda will counter that she, alone, was using the rental property, and therefore that property and any income, profits, or rents derived from it should be her SP because it was used primarily by her. This argument will fail because it is not an item of tangible personal property and thus was not an exception to the transmutation in writing rule.

Wanda's argument that the rental was a gift from CP to SP will fail.

Rents, Issues and Profits
The rents, issues, and profits of CP will be CP, and the rents, issues, and profits of SP will be SP.

Because the rental property is CP, any rental income that Wanda derives by renting it out (the facts are silent about whether she has a tenant) will be CP, and therefore will be subject to the equal division in kind rule. Half of rents must be therefore shared with Harry.

Equal Management and Control
Each spouse has equal ability to manage and control CP. However, this is subject to certain limitations. For instance, a spouse may not sell or encumber personal property in the home or CP clothing belonging to either spouse or children without consent of the other spouse.

Gifts of CP
Moreover, spouses may not make gifts of CP without the written consent of the other spouse. A spouse may void the gift upon finding out about it.

Harry will argue that he did not consent to Wanda sneaking off and using money from their joint savings account to purchase the rental property and take title in her name alone. He will argue therefore that he should be allowed to void this transaction within one year of finding out about it. He will also argue that he can void this transaction because Wanda disposed of the CP without his written consent.

Wanda will argue that because she has equal management and control of the property, she does not need his consent to purchase a rental property with money from their joint savings account because she has a community interest in both of their salaries, and therefore can do what she wants with the money given that she had equal withdrawal rights on the bank account. She will also argue that this was not a "gift" of CP because she got her substantial benefit of the bargain from it: namely, a rental in exchange for the funds.

Wanda, unfortunately, likely has the stronger argument here, and she did not need Harry's consent before purchasing the rental and he likely cannot void it and cause the seller to return any of the purchase price despite finding out about the sale/purchase within one year.

Breach of Fiduciary Duty

Spouses owe each other fiduciary duties similar to those of business partners. They owe each other the highest duty of good faith and to avoid self-dealing.

Harry will argue that Wanda breached her fiduciary duty to him as a spouse by going behind his back and taking their joint CP funds and buying a rental and titling it in her own name without his knowledge. He will argue that this breaches her duty of loyalty to him and that this act was not in good faith.

Harry likely has a strong argument here, and he may also argue that this lack of good faith should cause the court to deviate from the equal division in kind rule.

Conclusion

The rental is CP because it was purchased with earnings during marriage, which were held in the bank account which is CP, given that the prenup is likely invalid. Therefore, it will be subject to equal division in kind upon divorce and Harry and Wanda will each take 50% of the proceeds from the sale of the rental, assuming it is sold, and assuming the court does not find justification for deviating from this, in light of Wanda's lack of good faith and fair dealing when going behind Harry's back to purchase the rental.

4. The hospital bill

End of the Economic Community: Permanent Separation

The economic community begins during marriage, and ends upon permanent separation. Permanent separation is understood through physical separation plus an intent not to resume the marital relationship.

Separate Debts of Spouses

Debts acquired after permanent separation are SP and the debtor spouse will be liable to his creditors for such debt incurred.

Here, Harry will argue permanent separation occurred in 2016 per the facts when "Wanda moved out of the condo" demonstrating an intent to not resume the marital relationship, and therefore the hospital bill incurred is her SP and only she will be liable for it because the economic community had ended.

Wanda will argue that Harry had not yet evidenced an intent not to continue the marital relationship because he only filed for divorce after her surgery and therefore the economic community was still intact, and thus the debt is CP to be shared between both of them.

Harry has the stronger argument, because per the facts, Harry and Wanda had "permanently separated" prior to the surgery.

Necessaries of Life

Despite the general rule that debts incurred post-separation are the SP debt of the debtor spouse and that spouse only will be liable for that debt to creditors, there is an exception for the "necessaries of life" and debts incurred on their behalf post-separation but before divorce, because of the duty spouses owe to each other to take care of each other during marriage.

Wanda will argue that her surgery was an "emergency surgery for a medical condition," and therefore was a necessary of life similar to food and water. Harry will have a difficult time countering this, because a court is likely to hold that this is a necessary.

Therefore, despite Wanda being the debtor spouse, if she does not have sufficient SP to pay for the $50,000 hospital bill, the hospital can attach to the CP of either spouse, and Harry may also be required to pay for the debt using his SP, because of the duty owed to take care of one's spouse prior to divorce, even after separation for necessaries of life.

Conclusion

In sum, the condo is CP and subject to equal division, the bank account is CP and subject to equal division, the rental property is CP and subject to equal division unless the court finds that it should deviate from this rule because of Wanda's breach of her fiduciary duty, and the hospital bill, despite being Wanda's separate debt, is a necessary of life which Harry may be required to pay for with CP and/or his SP.

QUESTION 5: SELECTED ANSWER B

Harry and Wanda's Rights and Liabilities

California is a community property state. In a community property state, the marital economic community begins on the formation of a valid marriage, and ends with the death of a spouse, divorce, or permanent physical separation with intent of one spouse not to resume marital relations. Property, earnings, and debt acquired during the marriage is presumed to be community property. Property acquired by either spouse before the marriage, or at any time via gift, devise, or inheritance, is presumed to be separate property. Property acquired by the couple while living in a non-community property state, if it would be considered community property if acquired in California, is considered quasi-community property upon death of a spouse or divorce.

Valid Marriage

A valid marriage requires mutual consent, sufficient age (at least 18 years old) and legal capacity, and formalities, including a license and solemnization. Here, though the facts do not specify the details of Harry and Wanda's marriage, we can assume for the purposes of this question that they were validly married.

A valid marriage ends upon the death of a spouse, divorce, or physical separation of the spouses with intent of one spouse (or both) not to resume the marital relationship. Here, Harry and Wanda permanently separated and Wanda moved out of the condominium where they had been living together in 2016. Harry also filed a petition for dissolution of the marriage. These actions--the physical separation of the two and the petition for dissolution--indicate that the spouses intended to permanently separate and not resume the marital relationship in 2016.

Premarital Agreements

Before analyzing Harry and Wanda's rights and liabilities in specific pieces of property, we first must determine whether their premarital agreement is valid and effective. A premarital agreement may alter the couple's ownership status in property if it is valid. To be valid, a premarital agreement must be in writing and signed by both couples, though there does not need to be valid consideration exchanged. Additionally, the proponent of the premarital agreement (as of 2005) bears the burden of proving that the agreement was neither involuntary nor unconscionable at the time it was executed.

Voluntariness

To prove that the agreement was voluntary, the proponent of the premarital agreement must prove (1) that the other party was represented by independent counsel, or had knowingly waived in a separate, signed writing the rights to separate counsel after being fully informed of the advantages of such separate counsel, (2) that the other party, if not represented by independent counsel, was fully informed of the rights it was giving up, (3) that the agreement was not obtained by fraud, duress, or undue influence by one of the spouses, and (4) other factors that the court may think appropriate and just.

(1) Here, neither party was represented by independent counsel. Though the proponent of the premarital agreement may argue that the parties waived their right to independent counsel by saying, in a separate signed document, "We agree we do not need legal advice," it is not clear that this waiver was valid, because the parties likely were not fully informed of the advantages of obtaining legal counsel. It is possible that they could argue that they were both legally sophisticated--as evidenced by their knowledge that they needed a separate signed document to waive--but in the absence of additional evidence of this sophistication, a court would likely hesitate to enforce the agreement on this basis.

(2) Similarly, it is not clear from the writing signed by the parties--either the agreement

or the separate signed writing--that the parties were fully informed of the rights that they were giving up. Unless the proponent can produce evidence that the other party was fully informed, the court may decline to enforce the agreement.

(3) Here, the facts are unclear regarding whether there was fraud, undue influence, or duress. The party seeking to enforce the agreement would bear the burden of showing that these factors did not exist at the time the agreement was signed.

Unconscionability

To prove that the agreement was not unconscionable at the time it was executed, the proponent of the agreement would need to prove that the other party was fully informed of the assets and liabilities of the proponent party, or that the other party had waived such a right to full disclosure of the assets and liabilities of the proponent party, or that the other party actually knew or had reason to know of the assets and liabilities of the proponent party. In the absence of facts speaking to such disclosure, we assume that the agreement was not unconscionable for the purposes of this analysis.

Transmutation

Finally, in order to be a valid transmutation (agreement that changes the status of ownership of property), a premarital agreement or other agreement must expressly declare the intent of the parties--particularly the adversely affected spouse--to change the ownership status of property.

The spouse aiming to defeat the premarital agreement will argue that saying that "Wanda's[/Harry's] salary is her[/his] property" is insufficiently clear to demonstrate intent to make the property separate property because it does not use the word "separate." However, the other spouse will argue that the intent is clear. Since the earnings acquired during marriage would otherwise be community property, saying that it would be the earning spouse's property is sufficient to demonstrate the parties' intent to make it separate property. The court would likely agree with the latter argument, since the intent to change the ownership status is clear.

Ultimately, however, since there was no independent legal counsel and the parties were likely not fully informed of the rights they were giving up, the party opposing the premarital arrangement will likely be able to prevent it from being enforced on the basis that it was not voluntarily signed.

The Condominium

Source of Funds and Time of Purchase

Property acquired during marriage from community property funds is presumed to be community property. This presumption holds true even if the spouse takes title in his or her name alone. The general community property presumption may be rebutted by a preponderance of the evidence.

Here, Harry used his salary to buy a condominium in 2004. The condominium was purchased after the marriage, using Harry's salary. Assuming that Wanda were able to defeat the premarital agreement and prevent it from being enforced, Harry's salary earned during the marriage would be community property. As a result, property purchased with this salary, as the condominium was, would be community property.

The Community Property Presumption

Harry will argue that the condominium should be his separate property. He may succeed in this argument if he can rebut the community property presumption by a preponderance of the evidence. Harry will argue that his title to the property in his name alone indicates his intent that the property should be his separate property. This alone, however, is not sufficient evidence to rebut the general community property presumption. Harry may also argue that he used separate property funds earned from before the marriage to purchase the condominium in addition to some of his salary after the marriage. Harry may be able to prove that separate property funds were used to purchase the condominium by either directly tracing the funds used in the purchase to a separate property source (by showing that separate property funds were available and that he intended to use them in this purchase) or by indirectly tracing the funds via the exhaustion method (showing that community property funds commingled with separate property funds were exhausted by family expenses such that only separate property funds remained in the account that was used for the purchase). If Harry can succeed in this tracing, it will not change the status of the property, but Harry may be entitled to an equitable right of reimbursement for the separate property funds that he used in purchasing the property (without interest), and he may be entitled to a pro rata share of the property as separate property in proportion to the part of the purchase price paid with separate property funds.

However, in the absence of such evidence--and there is no such evidence suggested by the facts--we assume that Harry's salary referenced in the facts was earned between 2003 and 2004, and that it was thus community property.

The Special Presumptions

Harry may also argue that the Special Presumption of Title should be applied to the property. The Special Presumption of Title states that the property's title and the manner in which it is held is presumed to reflect the status of the property. But this presumption only applies at death, so it is inapplicable.

Instead, the Special Presumption that applies at divorce is the Special Community Property Presumption. This presumption states that any property jointly held by the spouses (as joint tenants or as tenants in common) is presumed to be community property at divorce. Wanda will likely argue that this presumption applies. Harry may attempt to defeat this presumption via clear and convincing evidence, which evidence (after 1984) must include an express statement in writing, demonstrating that the property should be held as separate property. To defeat the presumption, Harry would need to produce in addition to this express statement--and there does not seem to be such a statement referring to the condominium--evidence of the sort discussed three paragraphs above. Again, in the absence of such evidence, Harry would not be able to rebut the community property presumption.

There are no transmutations suggested by the facts (again, assuming that the premarital agreement is unenforceable) that would change the ownership status of this property.

Dispositions

Thus, again assuming that the premarital agreement is unenforceable, the condominium is likely community property.

Upon divorce, the equal division rule applies, and community property is divided evenly between the spouses. Thus, Harry and Wanda are likely each entitled to 50% of the value of the condominium.

The Joint Savings Account

Source of Funds and Time of Purchase

The joint savings account was created in 2005. Both Harry and Wanda deposited $5,000 from their salaries into the account. These deposits of $10,000 a year over the course of 10 years would likely amount to $100,000, plus whatever interest the account has earned in that time. This $100,000 stemmed from Harry and Wanda's salaries. Again assuming that the salaries were community property, because they were earned during the marriage and the premarital arrangement is likely unenforceable, this bank account and the $100,000 it contains is community property.

At divorce, the special community property presumption applies (see rule above). Since the bank account is held in both of their names--it is a joint account--it is presumed to be community property, and the income earned on the account is also presumed to be community property.

There is no transmutation affecting this joint account.

At divorce, community property is divided equally between the spouses. Thus, not addressing for the moment the funds removed from the account to pay for the rental property, which will be addressed below, Harry and Wanda are each entitled to 50% of the account. This would be $50,000 (plus half of the interest) to Harry, and $50,000 (plus half of the interest) to Wanda.

The Rental Property

Source of Funds and Time of Purchase

The rental property was purchased by Wanda in 2015, during the marriage. Wanda used funds from the joint account to purchase the property. Assuming that the funds in the joint account were community property, this would make the rental property presumptively community property, as it was acquired during the marriage with community property funds.

Wanda will argue that the rental property was held in her name and that it should thus be separate property. However, this is not enough to rebut the community property presumption. Additionally, the special presumption of title does not apply at divorce, only at death. So, unless she were able to enforce the premarital agreement, which she will likely not be able to do, Wanda will not be able to argue that the rental property is her separate property.

Breach of Fiduciary Duty

Spouses owe each other fiduciary duties. These duties include the duty to inform the spouse of the status of community property and the duty to obtain consent for major decisions affecting the disposition of community property. If a spouse violates his or her fiduciary duty to the other spouse, as a remedy, the other spouse may have his or her name added to the title of the affected property, the spouse may be entitled to a larger share of the community property, or, if the property was fraudulently concealed, the innocent spouse may request that the court order the other spouse to forfeit the property entirely to the innocent spouse.

Here, assuming the joint account was community property funds, Wanda may have breached her duty to obtain consent for major decisions. She did not notify Harry about using money from their joint account to purchase the rental property, and she took title in her name alone. It is possible that she also intended to keep the proceeds from this rental property, which would be community property themselves, for herself, which would be a violation of the duty of loyalty and highest good faith owed to her spouse. Since there is insufficient evidence of fraudulent concealment of this property, the court is not likely to order that Wanda forfeit the property entirely, but the court may award Harry a larger share of the community property as a result of Wanda's breach.

The rental property is thus community property. At divorce, it will be divided evenly between the two spouses, with Harry receiving a larger share as the court deems just due to Wanda's breach of her fiduciary duties.

The Hospital Bill

Debts of spouses acquired after permanent physical separation are generally the liabilities of the debtor spouse, with that spouse being responsible for the debt payment after divorce. However, even after separation, both the debtor and the non-debtor spouse may be personally liable for payments for the necessities of life of either spouse.

The court may divide liability for such debts according to each spouse's ability to pay.

The hospital bill was for an emergency surgery. Such an emergency surgery is a necessity of life, and, as such, both Wanda and Harry will be personally liable. Harry may have an equitable right of reimbursement for any of his funds used in payment for the hospital bill, however, if he can show that Wanda had separate property funds available at the time the hospital bill was paid.

At divorce, either Harry or Wanda may be personally liable for the hospital bill. Assuming that Wanda's $50,000 share of the joint account is still intact, she may have had funds available for the payment herself. If this is true, Harry may be entitled to an equitable right of reimbursement for his own funds used to pay the hospital bill. Any funds that he used that made up for funds that Wanda did not have available will not be reimbursed to Harry.

QUESTION 6

Len, an attorney, is a member of Equal Ownership Inc. (Equal), a nonprofit organization that seeks to help low-income families purchase homes throughout the state. Len does not represent Equal as an attorney. Equal helped to get a statute enacted that requires that all new residential developments contain a certain percentage of low-income housing.

ABC Development Corp. (ABC) is a corporation that wants to challenge the statute. Pat, the President of ABC, asked Len to represent ABC and Len agreed. Len does not personally agree with ABC's objective, but moves forward with the representation nonetheless by filing a complaint challenging the statute. Len personally thinks the statute is a good law and secretly hopes that ABC is not successful in its lawsuit.

During the course of Len's representation of ABC, Pat informs Len that he (Pat) has filed false reports with the State Environmental Protection Agency regarding the disposal of non-hazardous waste, and is planning to file another false report next month. Filing a false report makes a person and his or her employer liable for a substantial civil fine. Len does not take any action with respect to the impending filing of the false report.

What ethical violations, if any, has Len committed? Discuss.

Answer according to ABA and California authorities.

Attorney-Client Relationship

An attorney-client relationship is formed when the client reasonably believes it has been formed. The existence of an attorney-client relationship triggers numerous duties, including the duties of competence, confidentiality, loyalty, and fiduciary duties. Breaching one of these duties is a violation of the Model Rules and California Rules.

Here, ABC has hired Len (L) to represent them in an effort to challenge the residential housing statute. Thus, it is likely that they reasonably believe an attorney-client relationship exists. One has therefore been formed. The duties mentioned above now apply to this relationship, and any breach will be considered an ethical violation.

For similar reasons, L does **not** have an attorney-client relationship with Equal. Although he has helped them get the housing statute enacted, he does not represent them as an attorney. Thus, we may assume that Equal would not reasonably believe such a relationship existed. Even in the absence of a formal relationship, however, his association with Equal may raise other problems, as discussed below.

Corporation as a Client

An attorney may represent a corporation as a client. The corporation acts through its duly-appointed representatives, usually officers. However, the corporation, not the officers, is the actual client and the attorney must be careful not to provide legal information to the officers in a personal capacity or to mislead them into believing that the attorney represents them personally.

Here, ABC, a corporation, has retained L to handle the representation. This is permissible under both sets of rules. ABC, acting through Pat (P), will likely give L instructions on how to proceed and define what the goals of the representation are. However, L must remember that he represents ABC and not P.

Duty of Loyalty

An attorney owes his clients a duty of loyalty. The duty of loyalty includes the duty to refrain from conflicts of interest. Conflicts of interest take several forms: conflicts personal to the lawyer, conflicts between current clients, and conflicts between current and past clients.

Lawyer-Client Conflict

A lawyer may breach his duty of loyalty by representing a client with interests adverse to his own. This often arises when litigation the attorney is handling is adverse to one of his personal interests. When an attorney has a conflict between his or her personal interests and the interests of the client, under the California Rules he or she must provide the attorney with written disclosure of the interest. The model rules, by contrast, require that the attorney get informed consent from the affected client before continuing with a representation that raises a personal conflict. Further, under the Model Rules, the lawyer must reasonably believe that he will be able to provide competent and diligent representation in the face of the conflict.

Here, under either rule, L has breached his duty of loyalty. L is a member of Equal, an organization that helped to pass the statute his new client, ABC, is now challenging. L has admitted that he thinks the law is valid and that he hopes ABC is not successful in its suit. Under the Model rules, this would be a violation because he cannot reasonably believe he will be able to provide diligent and competent representation in the face of this admission. Further, under the California rules, there is no indication that he has provided written disclosure to ABC of his personal interest. He may argue that ABC only knew about him because of his work with Equal, and thus ABC was necessarily informed of his interest. However, California requires written disclosure, which was not provided. L has breached his duty of loyalty by representing a client in the face of a personal conflict without disclosure and without a reasonable basis for believing he can continue to provide competent and diligent representation.

Client Conflicts

A lawyer may breach his duty of loyalty by representing current clients with interests adverse to one another or by representing a current client whose interests are adverse to a former client.

Current Clients

A lawyer may breach his duty of loyalty by representing current clients whose interests are adverse to other current clients. Under the Model Rules, a lawyer must get informed consent from the adversely affected client and reasonably believe that they can undertake the representation in spite of the conflict. The Model Rules require this consent only for **actual** conflicts of interest. By contrast, California requires informed consent for either **actual** or **potential** conflicts of interest. However, California does not require that the attorney reasonably believe he can prove competent representation in the face of the conflict.

Here, although Equal might argue that there is a client conflict, it is unlikely that L has breached either the model or California rules by agreeing to represent ABC. L was a member of Equal, but there was never an attorney-client relationship between L and Equal. There would therefore be no need to get informed consent from ABC or Equal before pursuing the representation of ABC.

Former Clients

Like a conflict of interest arising from the representation of current conflicting clients, an attorney may likewise breach their duty of loyalty by representing a client with an interest adverse to a former client. In this case, the test under the California rules is generally whether the attorney learned any confidential information in the previous representation which could harm the client.

Here, like above, there is likely no former client conflict because there was no attorney-client relationship with Equal. However, Equal's argument on this front would be stronger--there is a strong possibility that as a lawyer-member of Equal, he learned information about Equal's litigation and lobbying strategies that could be used by ABC to defeat the statute. If he obtained confidential information from Equal, some courts might treat it as an ethical violation to use this information in subsequent litigation against that organization without getting informed consent. However, because there was no actual attorney-client relationship between Equal and L, it's unlikely that he breached his duty of loyalty by not getting Equal's informed consent.

Duty of Competence

An attorney owes a duty of competence to his client. Under both the Model rules and the California rules, this requires that he or she have the requisite knowledge, skill, thoroughness, and preparation necessary to handle the case. If a lawyer is not competent to handle the representation, he must become competent before proceeding, associate with a competent lawyer, or withdraw.

Here, although there is nothing to suggest that L is technically incompetent to represent ABC (he likely has experience in this area of law through his membership in Equal), it is possible that his affiliations and loyalties make it such that he cannot provide competent representation. He has admitted that he secretly hopes ABC is not successful in its lawsuit. This signals that he is biased against his client and therefore might be tempted not to use the requisite knowledge, skill, thoroughness, and preparation the representation deserves. If this is the case, then L will have breached his duty of competence to ABC.

Duty of Confidentiality/Disclosure

An attorney owes a duty of confidentiality to his clients. This requires, under both sets of rules, that they keep any information related to the representation confidential and inviolate. The duty of confidentiality is not absolute, and the Model rules and California rules both have exceptions for disclosure in case of fraud or financial harm (Model rules) or the threat of serious bodily harm or death (both sets of rules).

Here there are two potential issues related to confidentiality: (i) the possibility that L will breach his duty of confidentiality and provide information related to the representation of ABC to Equal, and (ii) whether L has a duty (or permission) to disclose information related to ABC's filing of false reports.

(i) Threat of Disclosure to Equal

As mentioned above, a lawyer must not disclose <u>any</u> information related to the representation to an outside source.

Here, his close association with Equal, a company whose law he is now attempting to strike down on behalf of ABC, presents a serious risk that he will violate the duty of confidentiality by disclosing information related to ABC's challenge of the law. Although there is no indication that he has yet made such a disclosure, if he does, he will have violated the duty of confidentiality and thus have committed an ethical violation.

(ii) Reporting ABC's False Reports

The Model rules and California rules treat the disclosure of confidential corporate information differently. When an attorney discovers that a corporation has undertaken an unlawful act, such as filing fraudulent documents or committing a criminal act, under both sets of rules an attorney must first **report up**. Reporting up requires that the attorney take the matter to the most senior member of the corporation. Under the

Model Rules, if the executives of the corporation refuse to take action, the lawyer may **report out** if he believes it is in the best interest of the corporation. This is an exception to the duty of confidentiality and allows the lawyer to report misconduct to an outside agency. California does not permit reporting out for financial crimes. California permits reporting out only when he or she has reason to believe that (i) the client or a third party will commit an act that creates a **risk of death or substantial bodily harm**, (ii) he or she has **remonstrated** the client to not take this action, and (iii) the disclosure is **reasonably necessary** to prevent the harm. Under the California rules, a lawyer may not disclose financial harms, although he may choose to withdraw from the representation.

Here, L has discovered that P has filed false reports with the State EPA regarding the disposal of non-hazardous waste and is planning to file another false report soon. Filing this false report opens the corporation up to a substantial civil fine. As a threshold matter, L should report this matter up the chain of command of the company. However, as it appears that P is the president, it is not apparent who else this could be reported to. Under the Model Rules, since L has exhausted his "reporting up" options, L is permitted to disclose the false report to an outside agency, since this involves a threat of substantial financial harm to the corporation. He may also withdraw from representation. He does not violate the Model Rules by not filing the report, although he may not counsel them on committing this type of fraud.

By contrast, L has no ability to report the fraud under the California rules. California permits reporting outside the corporation only where there is a risk of death or substantial bodily harm. The facts indicate that the waste is non-toxic, and thus it is unlikely that there is any risk of bodily harm. Although L may choose to withdraw from the representation and may not counsel the corporation on filing such documents, he is not required (or allowed) to disclose--to do so would be a breach of the duty of confidentiality.

In short, L's responsibilities in the situation depend on the rules applied. Under either circumstance, he can likely withdraw from the representation since the client is committing fraud. Under the Model Rules, he may, but is not required to disclose the fraud to an outside agency. Under the California rules, he may not disclose the fraud and would be liable for a breach of confidentiality for doing so.

Duty of Candor to the Court

In addition to duties owed to the client, an attorney also owes a duty of candor to the court. As part of an attorney's duty of candor to the court, the lawyer owes a duty not to advance or file frivolous claims under both the California and Model Rules. This requires that they not knowingly put forward a claim that is unsupported by the law, although a good faith argument for modification or reversal is not considered frivolous.

Here, L has filed a claim seeking to invalidate the residential housing statute, a law that he helped pass. He has admitted that he secretly hopes that ABC is not successful in its lawsuit and that the statute is good law. Thus, there is a substantial likelihood that he will violate the duty of candor by filing a suit seeking to invalidate the law. This is because, if the law is valid, then claiming it is not valid without a reasonable basis is considered a frivolous claim. L will argue that he does not <u>know</u> that the law is good law, he just believes it is. Therefore, because he does not <u>know</u> whether the law is good or not, he is not prohibited from putting forth a good faith argument that it should be modified or overturned. Whether this argument succeeds depends on whether or not he believes there is a good faith basis for challenging the law. If he does not, and he proceeds to litigate the claim anyway, he will have violated his duty of candor to the court.

QUESTION 6: SELECTED ANSWER B

DID LEN COMMIT ANY ETHICAL VIOLATIONS IN CHOOSING TO REPRESENT ABC?

Duty of loyalty

A lawyer owes to their client the duty of loyalty. Under the ABA rules, the duty of loyalty requires that a lawyer not take a representation when there is a conflict of interest, unless the lawyer: (1) reasonably believes that his ability to represent the client will not be materially limited by the conflict of interest; and (2) the lawyer discloses the conflict to the client and receives their informed consent to continue with the representation. The California rules are quite similar, except the lawyer only needs to have a good faith subjective belief that his ability to represent the client will not be materially limited by the conflict of interest, and if the conflict is a personal conflict, the lawyer only needs to provide a written disclosure of the conflict in writing to the client. However, if the conflict is not a personal conflict, the client's consent itself, and not just a confirmation of consent, must be in writing.

Conflict of interest #1: Len's membership of Equal Ownership Inc. (Equal)

Did a conflict of interest exist?

Although Len did not represent Equal, a conflict of interest still likely existed because Len was a member of Equal, yet he agreed to represent ABC in its suit to challenge the statute. Equal was the nonprofit organization that helped to get the statute in question enacted. As a member of Equal, Len likely assisted or at the very least approved of and supported Equal in its mission to help get the statute enacted. Now, Len is on the opposite side of the same conflict, seeking to get this same statute struck down.

Accordingly, Len had a conflict of interest due to his membership of Equal and his representation of ABC, as Len was required to essentially fight a statute that was supported by the nonprofit which he was a part of.

<u>Did Len take appropriate steps to represent ABC notwithstanding this conflict?</u>

ABA MODEL RULES

Under the ABA model rules, Len could still represent ABC notwithstanding this conflict if: (1) he reasonably believed his ability to represent ABC would not be materially limited by this conflict; and (2) Len obtained ABC's informed consent in writing. Note that Len was not required to obtain Equal's informed consent, because Len does not represent Equal as an attorney.

Here, Len would argue that Len could reasonably believe he could represent ABC notwithstanding this conflict because even though he was a member of Equal, Len did not necessarily participate in the specific lobbying strategies or otherwise directly work on/contribute to Equal's efforts to enact the statute. Len could argue that though he supported Equal's mission at the time, this past support would not undermine his ability to represent ABC, despite the fact that ABC's objectives sought to tear down this specific statute.

On the other hand, it could be argued that Len's belief was not reasonable. Len was a member of the organization that supported and helped to enact the low-income housing statute. It could be argued that it would not be reasonable for Len to believe he could represent ABC and somehow place his membership of Equal and his support of Equal in an "isolated mental box" in his mind, which would not affect his ability to represent ABC, because the interests directly and squarely conflict with one another.

Overall, Len may very well succeed on his argument that he reasonably believed that this conflict of interest would not have materially limited his ability to represent ABC. Len was only a member of Equal, and the facts do not suggest that Len spearheaded or otherwise was deeply involved with the Equal's work in helping the statute get enacted.

However, despite this fact, Len did not disclose the conflict to ABC at the time he chose to take on the representation. The facts do not suggest that Len told Pat he was a member of Equal, and that Pat consented to the representation notwithstanding this consent. Moreover, even if Len may have told Patrick about it and Patrick consented, such consent was not obtained or otherwise evinced by a writing.

Therefore, Len breached his duty of loyalty under the ABA model rules by improperly accepting a conflicted representation.

CA RULES

Here, Len would argue that he at the very least had a subjective good-faith belief that he could represent ABC notwithstanding his membership of Equal. A court would likely agree with Len, on grounds that as discussed above, while Len was a member of Equal, Len did not represent Equal, nor do the facts indicate that Len was directly or deeply involved with Equal's efforts to enact the statute. Accordingly, regardless of whether this belief was reasonable or not, Len may have had a good faith belief that he could have represented ABC notwithstanding this conflict.

However, Len did not provide a written disclosure of this conflict to ABC in writing. Indeed, this was a personal conflict, as it related to Len's membership with Equal and not some other conflict due to representation of other past or present client. However, under the ABA rules, Len was required to give ABC notice of this conflict and obtain its informed consent in writing. Len did not provide such a disclosure or obtain informed consent.

Therefore, Len breached his duty of loyalty under the ABA model rules by improperly accepting a conflicted representation.

Conflict of interest #2: Len's personal disagreement with ABC's objective

Did a conflict of interest exist?

In addition to being conflicted due to his being a member of Equal, another potential conflict of interest existed because Len did not personally agree with ABC's objective. Len personally thought that the statute was a good law, and secretly hoped that ABC was not successful in its lawsuit. Len's interests therefore directly diverged and conflicted with those of the objectives of his client. Accordingly, a conflict of interest also existed as regards Len's personal sentiments as to the merits of ABC's lawsuit, which Len was working on.

Did Len take the appropriate steps to accept the representation notwithstanding the conflict of interest?

ABA MODEL RULES

Len would argue that he reasonably believed that he could still represent ABC despite the fact that he did not personally agree with ABC's objectives, and believed that the statute was good law. He would argue that it is common for lawyers to personally disagree with their client's positions, but for them to nonetheless do the work as required and necessary to further their interests in the current matter.

However, it could be argued that Len's belief was not reasonable. Len's beliefs **directly and completely** diverged from that of his client's objectives. Such a strong, powerful belief, which even led Len to secretly hope that ABC was not successful in its lawsuit, would have inevitably affected Len's ability to represent ABC fully and to his utmost ability. Accordingly, it could be argued that due to the divergent disparity between his beliefs, and the objectives of his client, which even led him to essentially root for his client's failure, Len could not have reasonably believed he could represent ABC despite his personal beliefs.

A court would likely find that Len's belief that he could represent ABC effectively notwithstanding his personal beliefs was likely to be unreasonable. While it is common for a lawyer to disagree to an extent with the client's objectives, here Len was completely against them. The severity of his belief, and the likelihood of his personal sentiments materially impairing his ability to represent ABC is strongly evinced by the fact that he was rooting against his own client's victory.

Moreover, as discussed above, Len did not disclose such a conflict in writing to ABC, nor did Len obtain their informed consent.

Therefore, Len breached his duty of loyalty in accepting this representation with a conflict of interest.

CA RULES

Indeed, it is still possible that Len had a good faith subjective belief that he could represent ABC notwithstanding his strong feelings against their objective. However, as discussed above, Len did not disclose the nature of the conflict in writing.

Therefore, Len breached his duty of loyalty under the CA rules in accepting the representation with a conflict of interest.

Duty of competence

The duty of competence requires that a lawyer pursue a representation with the knowledge, skill, prudence, and effort that is reasonably required for the representation. Under the California rules, the lawyer only violates his duty of competence if he intentionally, recklessly, or repeatedly commits ethical violations.

ABA MODEL RULES

Under the ABA Model Rules, it could be argued that Len violated his duty of competence in choosing to represent ABC notwithstanding such a conflict. A lawyer acting with appropriate knowledge and skill would have been aware that Len faced multiple conflicts of interest, and should not have taken on the representation. A lawyer acting with sufficient prudence would have been aware of the risks that his ability to represent the client would have been limited, and that he would be subject to discipline for taking on such representation. On the other hand, it may be argued that even a lawyer with appropriate knowledge, skill, and effort would have taken on this representation, as they would have had sufficient knowledge and skill to further ABC's interests notwithstanding the conflict of interest.

Under the ABA Rules, it is likely that Len breached his duty of competence. He did not act with the proper prudence in representing ABC, given the conflicts of interests that had existed.

CA RULES

Under the CA Rules, it is possible that Len did not violate his duty of competence. Len may have failed to act without prudence in accepting such a conflicted representation, but the facts do not suggest that Len had intentionally acted or even recklessly acted incompetently. Rather, he may have merely been negligent in taking on this representation, and this would not have been sufficient to support a finding of a breach of the duty of competence in California.

Conclusion

Len may have violated his duty of competence under the ABA model rules, but likely did not violate the CA rules.

DID LEN COMMIT ANY ETHICAL VIOLATIONS IN FILING THE COMPLAINT ON BEHALF OF ABC?

Duty to avoid filing frivolous lawsuits with the court

A lawyer has a duty to the courts and the judicial system to refrain from filing frivolous lawsuits with the court. A lawsuit is frivolous if the suit as filed was not warranted by the current law, or by a good-faith argument for a change in the law.

Here, Len personally thought that the statute is a good law. Yet, he still filed the lawsuit challenging the suit. Thus, it could be argued that Len breached his duty to the courts to avoid frivolous lawsuits, as he filed the suit without a good-faith belief that the suit was warranted by existing law or by a good-faith argument for a change in the law. However, it could also be argued that Len did not breach this duty because while Len may have personally believed the statute is good law, there is a possibility that other precedent and jurisprudence would have provided a good argument to strike it down.

It is likely that a court will find that Len did not breach this duty to the court. The facts indicate that Len **personally** thought that the statute was **a good law.** The statute was not necessarily founded on solid principles and immune from attack on other legal grounds. Thus, though Len personally disagreed with the filing of the complaint, there are insufficient facts to establish that it was frivolous to do so.

DID LEN COMMIT ANY ETHICAL VIOLATIONS FOR HIS FAILURE TO TAKE ACTION WITH RESPECT TO THE IMPENDING FILING OF THE FALSE REPORT?

Duty to protect the interests of the corporate client

When the lawyer represents a corporate client, the lawyer owes a duty to act in the corporate client's best interests. The duty to corporate clients provides that if the lawyer learns that the corporation, or one of its agents or employees, were to commit an act of wrongdoing or other act that would be harmful to the corporation's interests, or be imputed to the corporation to expose it to liability, the lawyer has a duty to report such information to the highest authority in the corporation, such as the corporation's CEO or Head of Counsel. If such reporting is not possible, or would not be effective at preventing the harm, under the ABA model rules, the lawyer **may** report the information to an outside authority to avoid **harm** to the corporation. In California, however, although internal reporting is still required, reporting to an outside organization is **not permitted** except when necessary to comply with the requirements of the Sarbanes-Oxley Act.

Len **may** have breached his duty to the corporation under the ABA and California model rules. Here, Len found out that Pat had filed false reports with the State Environmental Protection Agency (EPA), and that Pat is planning to file another false report next month. Len was also aware that filing a false report makes a person **or his or her employer** liable for a **substantial civil fine.** Accordingly, Len was aware that one of the employees of his client (ABC), had taken actions, and was going to take actions, that could both be **imputed** to the corporation, AND would expose the corporation to liability. Therefore, Len was required to "run the information up the corporate flagpole."

The facts do not indicate whether Pat was the highest authority in ABC or not. Indeed, Pat was ABC's president. However, it is possible that there were other corporate officers (i.e., a CEO or something) or directors that were higher up on the "corporate flagpole" than Pat. If there were such individuals available, Len was required to inform them of Pat's actions to avoid having civil liability imputed to his client, ABC, and his client being subject to potential civil liability by having to pay a fine. Assuming that there were other individuals who were higher up than Pat on the corporate flagpole, Len may have violated his duty to protect the corporation's interests in failing to take any action with respect to the impending filing of the false report.

Note that under the ABA Model rules that if, however, Pat was the highest authority at ABC, Len was **permitted, but not required** to disclose the information regarding the false report to the State Environmental Agency. Len was not mandated to disclose, but only was permitted to do so. Accordingly, under these circumstances, because Len did not have an affirmative duty to disclose, but only had the right and the privilege to disclose to an outside authority, Len did **not** breach his duty to protect the corporation's interests by failing to report the false reports to the State EPA.

Conclusion

Therefore, Len **may** have breached his duty to protect the interests of his corporate client under the ABA and California rules, depending on whether there were other individuals on the "corporate flagpole" that Len could have reported this information to in order to protect the corporation from having liability imputed onto it by an action of one of its employees.

Duty of confidentiality - was disclosure required or permitted in these circumstances?

Because Len was not required to disclose the information to the State EPA due to his duties to protect the interests of his corporate client, the only other means by which Len may be disciplined is if he was **required** to make such a disclosure and breach his duty of confidentiality.

A lawyer owes to his clients a duty of confidentiality. The duty of confidentiality requires that a lawyer may not disclose or reveal any information that the lawyer receives as part of the representation. The duty of confidentiality continues even after the representation has ended, and even after the death of the client.

Under the ABA model rules, the lawyer is **permitted** to reveal confidential information from the client in the following circumstances: (1) Where necessary to avoid serious bodily injury or death to others; (2) Where necessary to avoid or ameliorate financial injury to others that was a result of crime or fraud that was accomplished with the lawyer's services; (3) Where reasonably necessary to further the representation; and (4) Where reasonably necessary to comply with other ethics obligations, such as the disclosure of limited client information for conflicts checks. In California, however, the lawyer is only permitted to disclose confidential information to avoid physical injury or death to others, **and** if reasonable, before disclosure, the lawyer must first: (1) reason with the client and attempt to persuade him not to follow through with his acts AND (2) tell the client of his intent to disclose.

Avoid serious bodily injury or death

Here, Pat had filed false reports with the State EPA regarding the disposal of **non-hazardous waste.** While ABC may have been improperly disposing waste, such waste was non-hazardous. Therefore, it is likely that the disclosure of this confidential information was not reasonably necessary to avoid serious bodily injury or harm, as the waste was not hazardous waste.

Moreover, even if the waste was hazardous, the lawyer's duty to disclose was **permissive, and not mandatory.** Accordingly, Len did not breach his duty of confidentiality under either the ABA or CA rules, as this exception was not applicable, and Len was **permitted, but not required** to provide such disclosure.

Avoid financial injury to others due to crime/fraud procured through use of lawyer's services

Here, Len's representation concerned challenging the low-income housing statute. However, Pat's statements to Len were completely unrelated to the scope of his representation and provision of legal services, as Pat's false reports were related to the disposal of non-hazardous waste, and false reports in connection with such disposal to the EPA.

Though the disposal of non-hazardous waste may have harmed other individuals' financial interests, as the non-hazardous waste may have caused damage to others' property, such harm was not procured using Pat's legal services. Moreover, as with the duty to disclose information to prevent physical injury or death, the duty to disclose to avoid financial injury is also **permissive,** rather than mandatory.

Therefore, even if this rule was applicable, Pat did not violate any duty in failing to report or disclose this information, as his duty to disclose was **permissive,** not mandatory. Note, moreover, that California does not have this exception.

Conclusion

Len was not required to disclose the information regarding the filing of the false report in the present case. Although he may have been permitted to do so under two exceptions to the duty of confidentiality under the ABA Model Rules, Len was not required to do so.